I0450674

What Freedom Is

What Freedom Is

Wells Earl Draughon

Writer's Showcase
New York Lincoln Shanghai

What Freedom Is

All Rights Reserved © 2003 by Wells Earl Draughon

No part of this book may be reproduced or transmitted in any form or by any means, graphic, electronic, or mechanical, including photocopying, recording, taping, or by any information storage retrieval system, without the written permission of the publisher.

Writer's Showcase
an imprint of iUniverse, Inc.

For information address:
iUniverse, Inc.
2021 Pine Lake Road, Suite 100
Lincoln, NE 68512
www.iuniverse.com

ISBN: 0-595-26619-3 (pbk)
ISBN: 0-595-65613-7 (cloth)

Printed in the United States of America

Contents

The Crisis in the Meaning of Freedom

Freedom has always been of the highest importance to Americans and to every other people who have had a taste of it. We do not need to be persuaded of its value. We sense that it is bound up with the quality of our personal lives; and we use it explicitly to judge the actions of our government: If the actions promote or protect our freedom, we favor them. To put it mildly: we feel strongly about this word. If our freedom is threatened too severely, we will fight to defend it. We have done so in the past. No one would dare openly attack an ideal so strongly defended.

What is happening, though, is that the *concept* of freedom, the meaning the word has for all of us, is being undermined. This has been going on for some time now, and the specialists who deal in such abstract regions—political theorists, political philosophers and legal theorists—are well aware of it. For instance, Lon Fuller wrote some years ago that "the concept of freedom has been undergoing a progressive deterioration and dissipation of meaning." If this process of dissipation of meaning proceeds much further, we will no longer be able to cry that a proposed governmental policy violates our freedom, because "freedom" will not mean what it used to mean. Already this objection is weakened by the fact that the meaning of the word is so fundamentally in dispute.

Why is this happening?

There are several reasons. Freedom is one of those words that has a "cash value" as it were. If you are trying to get the government to adopt a particular policy, you can claim that freedom will be one of the outcomes of the policy. Or if a law already passed is under attack, you can defend it by claiming that it promotes freedom. Partisans seek to get this word on their side.

Since the debate is always in terms of *predicted* outcomes ("I'm sure freedom *will result* from this policy"), it is easy to make claims of this kind: predicted outcomes are in the future. Still, sometimes it just isn't easy for the general public to swallow the claim that this or that law is going to increase freedom. Sometimes in fact, common sense suggests it will do exactly the opposite.

What can the partisans do to get their bill passed? Freedom is too well established for them to attack it directly. Partisans who are going to benefit from a set of government projects need to emasculate the word freedom so that it cannot be used against these projects. The way to do that is by arguing that the word freedom does not really mean what people think it means.

This scenario suggests a set of malicious partisans out to do in everybody else. Can we really believe that? Actually, it does not matter. If the concept of freedom is in disarray, then partisans can claim that their policies lead to it and that the other interest group's policies lead away from it.

Some of the disarray came about quite innocently. One way human knowledge has made progress over the centuries, when faced with complex or unclear concepts, is by analysis. To analyze a concept is to show that it is equivalent to several other concepts that are either simpler or clearer or less problematic. But when those other concepts are as problematic as the original concept, we have not made progress. Not only have we not made progress, but we have generated several additional problems: we now need an analysis of each of the new concepts in order to understand what *they* mean, and then we have to show how all these new concepts fit together.

This is one of the things that has happened to the concept of freedom.

But there is another cause that has led to the attempts to dilute the meaning of freedom. For some people, talk of freedom has always generated a sense of insecurity. After all, liberty was used as a battle cry in the revolt of the American colonists against the British. More seriously, liberty was a goal of the French Revolution.

Besides this, for other people—those who have the advantage over the rest of us in that they know with absolute certainty what is right and what is wrong—freedom has always raised the danger of "sin." Some people use their freedom to do things we don't think they ought to do. Apparently then, freedom itself is not necessarily a good thing.

This question whether freedom is a good thing has troubled a number of people. On the one hand, when it is *my* freedom that is in question, freedom is undoubtedly a good thing. When it is *your* freedom, then I'm not so sure. Similarly, when I, in exercising my freedom, do something stupid or do something I know to be wrong, it is not my freedom I blame, but my lack of information or lack of will power or Satan or circumstances beyond my control. But when *you* do something stupid or wrong, I begin to wonder whether you should have been allowed the freedom to do it in the first place.

Some people have, therefore, wanted to have it both ways: they have wanted to say that freedom is a good thing and they have wanted to say that people ought to do what is right. How can one have it both ways? You guessed it: By defining the word "freedom" in such a way that "freedom" *means* doing the right thing.

But has anybody really done that? Yes. And it began soon after the word freedom was introduced into practical politics. In the late seventeenth century, John Locke held that the three fundamental human rights were life, liberty and property. The counter-attack was not long in coming, and it came in the form of a re-definition of liberty. Montesquieu wrote: "In governments, that is, societies directed by laws, liberty can consist only in the power of doing what we ought to will and not being constrained to do what we ought not to will." Even Rousseau, who's most widely known remark is "Man is born free, yet he is everywhere in chains," sought to make his stress on freedom palatable to the powers of his society by writing: "To obey the laws laid down by society is to be free."

But when it was seen that society did not collapse as people acquired more freedom, the attack on liberty subsided for awhile. The rising new class of industrialists and entrepreneurs gave the word their support. And the framers of the American constitution could not well leave it out altogether since it had been one of the battle cries of the revolution.

In fact, by the time Mill wrote his famous essay on liberty in the middle of the nineteenth century, the idea of defining liberty did not even occur to him. Everyone knew what it meant and its meaning was not in dispute. He was writing to argue in favor of the benefits of liberty and to discuss the problem of the conditions under which a society could legitimately limit a person's freedom (a problem we shall be much concerned with here also). He needed only to remind his readers in passing that "liberty consists in doing what one desires." In other words, the common sense notion of freedom was completely adequate as far as Mill was concerned.

What happened?

As philosophers after Mill began to discuss liberty in more detail, it appeared that there were problems with the common sense definition. Consider the follow argument:

> Freedom is good.
> Sometimes people, in doing what they want, do bad things.
> Therefore, freedom cannot *mean* doing what you want.

In more concrete terms, Smith wants to kill Jones and does so. Since killing is not a good thing, and since Smith wanted to kill, how can freedom mean doing what you want?

An argument like this makes it look as though we must either stop saying freedom is a good thing or stop saying freedom is doing what you want to do.

For some thinkers, the solution was to define freedom as doing something good. "For man is not free but enslaved when he seeks merely the satisfaction of his own unrestrained desires. He becomes free when and insofar as he endeavors to act as a moral being." Those who propose such a re-definition of liberty are criticized, of course. Oppenheim, for example, calls this version of freedom "desirable unfreedom."

Think about this for a minute. We started out trying to define what freedom means and we have ended up prescribing what people should do and telling them they are not free unless they do as we say. The definition of "freedom" has been turned upside down. It has been defined as exactly the opposite of what it originally meant!

Well, maybe that only means that we have made progress in recent years.

What is wrong, of course, is that our freedom—that ability to do as we please which we so prize—has been taken away from us. With this new definition, we still have something called "freedom", but we no longer have the right to do what we want.

Well, we may not like it, but that doesn't prove it is wrong. How are we going to get around that argument above that led to this problem?

When people use their freedom to hurt other people, most of us agree that certain limits ought to be set to their freedom. But if freedom is a good thing, how can it be good to limit it?

This apparent paradox dissolves as soon as we look more closely at a particular case: If Smith uses his freedom to hurt Jones, then Jones's freedom has been curtailed by Smith's action. What Jones wants is not to be hurt by Smith. To allow Smith to hurt Jones is, therefore, to allow the limitation of Jones's freedom.

What we have here, in other words, is not a question of whether it is good to limit Smith's freedom, but *whose* freedom is going to be limited, Smith's or Jones's. In other words, we have a conflict of liberties. A theory of how to resolve conflicts of liberties is as important as a theory of liberty itself. Or, to put it more generally, we need a theory of what the limits of freedom should be.

But there are good reasons for not trying to build this limitation into the *definition* of freedom. When we keep the meaning of "freedom" separate from the question of the advisable limits to freedom, we can say that "such and such is what I mean by freedom; however, freedom ought to be limited in various ways." In other words, we first define "freedom" and then say under what conditions it is justifiable to limit it. A person who exceeds these limits can still be described as free but is said to have misused his or her freedom or simply to have done something wrong.

This is different from saying that unless a person's behavior is limited in this or that way, it simply *is not* "freedom." Saying it this way requires us to say that a person who exceeds one of the limits has suddenly (by definition) ceased to be free. Such an approach would lead easily to such locutions as: "to be free is to stay within the limits," or "to exceed the limits is slavery," etc. This is the sort of talk George Orwell called "doublethink".

Another argument for clearly separating the definition of liberty from a theory of the limits to liberty is this: Suppose a man commits a crime because someone is holding a gun at his back and forcing him to do it. Because the man was not free when he committed the crime, he could not be held responsible for committing it. In other words, freedom is a necessary condition for responsibility. Now, if we were to set up the definition of freedom in such a way that any person who transgressed the prescribed limits was by definition "not free", then a man who voluntarily committed a crime would be "not free" when he committed the crime (since crime is beyond the limits). Therefore, he could not be held responsible for committing it. In other words, people could not be held responsible for any actions they engaged in beyond the prescribed limits, since they were not "free" at the time.

But these sound like rather abstract difficulties. Are there any practical reasons for not building the notion of limits to freedom into the meaning of freedom?

Yes, and they are even more serious. Embedding the notion of limits to liberty in the concept of liberty *without saying what those limits are* effectively destroys the value of liberty as an ideal. How so? It puts us in the following situation: Whenever a person's freedom is interfered with, those doing the interfering can always say, "Oh yes, but that is one of the limits of liberty." And people could never defend their freedom to do **x**, since opponents could always claim that doing **x** exceeds the limits to freedom. This is the situation we are in at present.

Besides all this, there are other practical reasons for clearly distinguishing between freedom and the limits to freedom: the question where ought the limits of liberty to be set is a more difficult and more controversial one than the question what is liberty. By separating the two questions, we make it easier to find a concept of liberty that can be agreed upon.

So, a theory of limits to liberty is needed. But how can you develop a theory of the limits of freedom until you have said what freedom is? And to try to develop a theory of limits with only a vague definition of freedom or an unspecified one may result in more constraints on freedom than the theory of limits anticipates. By contrast, a more detailed and adequate concept of freedom may actually aid the task of developing an adequate theory of limits.

◆   ◆   ◆

But trying to hide a theory of limits to freedom inside the meaning of freedom is not the only challenge to our liberty. There are those who want the meaning of the word freedom restricted to "non-interference." In this conception, "freedom" means nothing more than *not being prevented* from acting.

Philosophers have labeled this conception "negative freedom". By contrast, defining freedom as "ability to do what you want" is dubbed "positive freedom." This splitting in two of the word freedom then leads naturally to a debate over which is the right meaning of the word, "negative freedom" or "positive freedom". And this is exactly what has happened. In fact, this debate is carried on with great passion on both sides.

Why? Why are two groups, both claiming to be strongly in favor of freedom, attacking each other?

The situation becomes even more puzzling when you stop to think about "negative freedom." Why is *anyone* strongly in favor of it? If being free merely means not being interfered with, then if you fell on the sidewalk and broke your leg and nobody interfered with you but left you there to starve, you would be said to be completely free. If this is all freedom means, who would adopt it as a goal of society, let alone fight to keep it? What is going on here? Who would ever argue in favor of adopting such an emasculated concept of liberty?

The puzzle dissolves, however, when you realize who the partisans are. Those arguing in favor of "negative freedom" are business organizations and their sympathizers. "Non-interference" means that government should not interfere with their business practices.

What has happened here is that some people have first selected which policies they favor and then changed the definition of freedom to fit those policies.

In addition to favoring such government policies, these partisans are afraid that if liberty means "positive freedom", someone will argue (as many do) that poor people are not very free, since poor people cannot do very much of what they want to do (since they cannot afford it). The government should promote freedom. Therefore…Heavens! It seems as if "positive freedom" might justify the Welfare State!

But this is not a necessary consequence of "positive freedom". What policies a society should adopt to maximize the freedom of its citizens is a complex question. It is by no means obvious that a welfare state is the best such policy. Also, since welfare for the poor must be paid for by the middle class, the freedom of people in the middle class is being decreased (or limited). We have, then, a situation of conflicts of liberties; and this is to be settled, not by changing the definition of freedom, but by developing and defending a theory of the limits of liberty and by figuring out how a society can contribute to maximizing *everyone's* freedom.

Recent developments in political theory have not been carried on entirely by those who are opposed to liberty, of course. Some thinkers have already begun attempting to integrate these two opposed definitions into a single concept of liberty. For example, they have argued that the distinction between "positive" and "negative" liberty has been maintained by arbitrarily restricting the range of constraints considered. Feinberg, by eliminating these restrictions, shows one possible synthesis of the two conceptions. (See Notes.)

◆   ◆   ◆

But the splitting of the meaning of freedom into two opposed definitions is not the only way the concept has been splintered. Picking up terms from ordinary political discourse (terms like "freedom of speech", "freedom of the press", etc.), some theorists have set about the task of defining *them* (without having defined freedom *per se*). The decision to start with these expressions as single unified concepts creates problems that we would not otherwise have, problems such as: What is the relation between freedom of the press and freedom of assembly? Or between any other of these types of freedom? Which of these types of freedom is more important? There is even a tendency to *equate* freedom with these particular activities (such as freedom of speech, freedom of press, freedom of assembly.)

We can understand the motivation behind these definitions. With the above debates raging, some people want to make sure that we remain free to do at least certain types of activities (like speak, publish and assemble). Since, as we have seen, freedom must be limited somewhere and no theory of limits exists, it is realistic to be afraid that freedom to do these activities might be limited or eliminated.

This strategy, though, has led to a field-day of equating "liberty" with various activities or outcomes or even political structures which the theorist is in favor of. For example, we have the term "economic freedom." We have "freedom as satisfaction of basic needs." We have "freedom as government by consent."

But this is the wrong way to go about trying to defend liberty. For one thing, these efforts are too easy to refute: If liberty is equated to a list of specific activities, then all behaviors not included on the list would have to be considered "non-free" (by definition).

One can attempt to avoid this problem by attaching adjectives to the word "freedom", as in "political freedom" or "economic freedom". But this move only creates pseudo-problems like: What is the relation between political freedom and economic freedom? Which has priority? Worse still, it does not even solve the problem. Other *political* activities could be found that were not included in the list to which "political freedom" was equated and you would have to be called "unfree" if you did any of these activities. And the same is true of "economic freedom" and all the other *types* of freedom that have been invented.

Another problem with such views is that the definitions contain an implicit theory of limits to liberty, hence, they are subject to the objections raised above against embedding a theory of limits into a concept of freedom. The limits these definitions imply are restrictions on behavior incompatible with the activity favored by the inventors of these definitions. For example, the definition of economic freedom or freedom of enterprise might rule out strikes by unions. Striking unions in such a conception would not simply be exercising *their* freedom but would be *interfering* with "economic freedom."

◆   ◆   ◆

Unfortunately, I have not yet revealed to you all of the attempts to reduce our freedom by changing the meaning of the word. There are others, perhaps more insidious than the ones considered so far. For instance, some of the most prestigious authors writing on liberty recently have claimed that only conditions imposed by human agency are relevant to freedom. Berlin says, "You lack political liberty or freedom only if you are prevented from attaining a goal by human beings. Mere incapacity to attain a goal is not lack of political freedom." More generally, Scott says, "Inability that is not the result of a conscious human intention to render us unfree…does not raise the question of freedom." And Oppenheim in spite of qualifications seems to concur.

But Mary, going about her daily business and cherishing her individual freedom, might well be made uneasy by such sophistication. In her common-sense way, she might wonder: Suppose a person locks me in a room by accident rather than with a "conscious intention" to limit my freedom. Does this mean that, even though I am *locked* in a room, I am really still free?

The authors who invented this position are aware of such awkward consequences of their re-definition of freedom but have had difficulty bringing themselves to shout through the locked door to inform Mary that she is still free. Instead, Scott says that the word "freedom" becomes "inapplicable" to situations of this sort, while von Hayek speaks of the word's applying only "figuratively": "…if that same climber were to fall into a crevasse and were unable to get out of it, he could only figuratively be called 'unfree'…". If I understand von Hayek's position, however, if the climber had been pushed into the crevasse (by a human, not by his horse), the person's unfreedom would be literal, not figurative.

If these views are adopted, then it is not the features of the situation we are in that determine how free we are but how the features got there, what caused them. In such a society, a woman would not know whether she were free or not until she found out whether the various conditions preventing her from doing what she wanted to do were caused by human beings. And since she wouldn't be able to prove she was unfree, she couldn't protest. Consider indirect causation, for instance: if a previous hiker accidentally loosened a stone that caused a later climber to fall into his imprisoning crevasse, is the latter person then unfree? Or free? Most physical as well as social conditions are influenced to some degree by many factors past and present. The applicability of the word "freedom" would be in doubt in many if not most cases.

But why should we accept this re-definition of freedom? Who cares how the conditions got there? The fact remains that a person who becomes imprisoned in a cave as a result of a cave-in *is* nonetheless imprisoned. To claim that the word "freedom" is inapplicable to this situation or that the person's unfreedom is only figurative is to compromise the word "freedom" to an extreme degree!

I know what you're wondering: These theorists are in *favor* of freedom? *Americans* wrote these things?

What these theorists seem to be afraid of is this: they are developing a theory of liberty to use in discussions of public policy. No one wants to be committed by a theory of liberty to requiring the government to regulate cave-ins or to pass laws governing falls into crevasses. To allow the term liberty to apply to conditions like this *might* lead to such absurd consequences. Hence, (they seem to feel) we have to keep them out by definition.

But we do not need to say that governments should adopt any and all possible policies if they would increase anybody's liberty to any extent. This would be economically unfeasible. Priorities have to be established. Establishing priorities is difficult, but again, ruling out certain policies *by definition* makes such possible policies unavailable for discussion.

◆   ◆   ◆

Another way of eliminating our freedom by a skillful re-definition is to claim that freedom is entirely subjective. Whether a person is free depends on whether the person feels free. For those philosophers who take a non-committal approach, this has become merely another *type* of freedom and is given the label "subjective freedom".

But while it is true that it must be possible to experience freedom subjectively, to define freedom as a mere perception quite apart from the real world is dangerous at best. It is possible for people to be mistaken about their freedom, especially if, for example, they have been taught from infancy certain beliefs about freedom, such as that freedom means following orders. For these reasons, liberty cannot be restricted to subjective perception alone.

Of course, subjective experience is important, and a willingness to confront one's own experience quite apart from pre-existing theories of what does and does not constitute freedom can be useful as a touchstone to test the relevance of any proposed dimension of the concept of liberty.

◆   ◆   ◆

Finally, we must mention what is certainly the most serious restriction on the meaning of freedom. This one, however, cannot be blamed on any particular theorist and did not come about recently. It was inherited from the past. Freedom is conceived of as "all or nothing": a person is either completely free or not free at all.

We are so used to thinking of freedom this way that it seems natural, even obvious. Nevertheless, this aspect of our concept of freedom is not only restrictive, but dangerous. A complete absence of freedom may be as difficult to find as a complete absence of heat. Even "Stone walls do not a prison make," since the mind is still free. Hence, we could be judged to be "free" rather than "unfree" in even the most confining situations, and we could not protest that our "freedom" had been taken away.

But there is another reason this categorical conception is so restrictive: far fewer conditions appear *relevant* to freedom when the question is whether a person is free or not free. Look at the cave-in example again. While we are debating whether the person trapped in the cave is free or not free, the debate can see-saw back and forth. Because we are being asked to draw a line. On one side of the line, a person is "free". On the other side, a person is "not free". Sometimes it seems reasonable to draw the line here; at other times, there.

But if we were to ask, Is a person outside the cave "more free" than the person trapped inside the cave? most people would not hesitate a minute. No one would say that the person outside is "just as free as" the person trapped inside. (Or if they would, this would show how deep the crisis in the concept of liberty had become.)

A comparative concept of liberty is, therefore, far more sensitive and thus more useful than a categorical one. As we shall see again and again throughout this book, cases that are difficult or impossible to solve when the categorical question is asked (free or not free) become almost trivially easy to solve when the question is asked in the comparative way (more free or less free).

Empirical research has shown that people do not balk at using a concept of "more free" and that in fact in at least some cases they agree in their application of the concept. Hence, the concept cannot be regarded as idiosyncratic of one or another author. Also, more of the conditions of liberty appear relevant to people when they must make the finer discrimination of "more free" than appear relevant in the categorical type of analysis. Such empirical studies cannot be regarded as supporting a claim that the comparative concept of liberty is the one that ought to be adopted, but they do make it impossible to throw out such a conception as absurd or meaningless.

In the comparative analysis, all free situations do not get lumped together indiscriminately as though they were equally free, and border-line cases do not have to be consigned forever to one of the two diametrically opposed categories "free" or "not free." The first advantage is the more important one because the comparative analysis makes it possible to ask—not just "Are people free?"—but "Are people as free as they can be? Should they be more free?" In other words, in the categorical analysis the task of policy is to provide it (freedom) for everyone (thereby ignoring possible differences between people in their degree of freedom). In the comparative analysis, the policy objective is to provide the *optimal level* of freedom for everyone. (What that level should be is a subject of one of our later chapters.)

What is Freedom?

Is it possible to come up with a definition of freedom that both avoids splintering its meaning and at the same time is not vulnerable to the objections raised against freedom in the last chapter?

This is what we want to achieve. But how are we to go about dealing with a word which seems so "high level" (that is, so abstract) and whose meaning seems to apply to so many different situations (that is, a word that is so general) as the word "freedom?" Shall we rush in and start talking about voting, about seat belts, about consumer sovereignty?

We could, and most theorists do; but we would find, as they have found, that answers to so many underlying issues have been presupposed, so many policies, wise or not, have been implicitly endorsed, the meanings of so many key terms have been taken for granted—that quite reasonable people could reasonably disagree with us and neither we nor they would have the faintest idea of all the places from which our disagreements originally stem. We would argue on and on, and each perceive the other to be, not only an imbecile, but possibly malevolent as well.

A more promising procedure is to start with extremely simple, even ridiculously oversimplified, situations and complicate them more and more, so that disagreements will arise one at a time and we will know when they arise and will know what we are disagreeing about. In this way, we do not get flooded at the start with a multitude of details, qualifications and complications.

◆   ◆   ◆

Note: Quibbles, asides and additional information
Given the extreme confusion over the meaning of "freedom", disagreements and questions are inevitable even in these simple situations.
And some people refuse to read further until these arguments are discussed. But pausing to discuss every objection that anyone has ever
thought of would make the main points impossible to follow. The way
out I've chosen is to put the answers to some of these arguments in
notes like this one. For the rest, you'll have to trust that I will deal with
them at some point in the book. Skip these boxes the first time through
and read them after having read the chapter.

◆   ◆   ◆

Even in constructing these simplified situations, we must not lose
sight of the real world, because after we have sorted out as many as we
can of the conditions defining freedom in these simple situations, we
must then move to real situations and show that our results still apply.
After that, we must deal with the additional complications that occur
in these real situations.

In constructing these simplified situations, we shall in this chapter
be using a method developed by philosophers called "analysis." That is,
we shall be trying to tease out the components of the meaning of "freedom." And we must do this without losing sight of the whole.

Let's begin, then, by constructing a variety of isolated situations,
each more complicated than the last, and asking what conditions,
found in these situations, make a person more free or less so.

Freedom in a single situation

Suppose we have a person, Mary. We say nothing for the moment
about where Mary is, what objects lie around her, or whatever. We

shall bring these factors in gradually to complicate the situation we are examining. But suppose, for the moment, that she is simply standing against a background of white seamless paper.

In one case, Mary has to stand there. In the other case, Mary can either stand there or not, as she pleases.

If Mary lacks this minimal degree of choice, that she can either do something or not do it, then we can safely say that this situation falls completely outside what we think of when we use the word "freedom." A person who does not have this choice *has* to do the action in question, even if the "action" is merely to keep standing there.

Let's look at a different example to illustrate choice.

Suppose we have a situation—a rather science-fiction type of situation—in which a man named Bill is doing something he enjoys doing, let's say he's playing Bridge. An instant later, Bill is doing something else he likes to do, work in his flower garden. In the next instant, Bill is doing something else he likes to do. Bill never knows when he will be doing something else or what he will be doing; but unlike the hero of **Slaughterhouse Five**, Bill does know that it will be one of the things he likes doing. It is not even Bill's mind that is controlling where he will be next. He has no control over it at all.

Now, imagine Bill in a situation in which he goes through exactly the same sequence of activities at exactly the same times—only now Bill *chooses* the times and the activities. Bill is as *well off* in the first situation as in the second; but in the second he is free, in the first he is not.

◆   ◆   ◆

Note: Awareness of choice

We ignore, for the moment, the extent to which Mary is aware of making a choice. If Mary takes a notion to play the piano, typically she simply goes to the piano and starts playing. She doesn't appear to make a decision. But such a choice is implicit in her behavior. She did not just stand there, she did something. People are usually aware of making a choice only when there are close competing alternatives of some importance and they are unsure which they prefer. Sometimes, people avoid making a choice because they don't want to think about it. They grab the first alternative that occurs to them and ignore the rest. This is probably just as well when the alternatives are to play the piano or to read, because the difference in value between the two for the person is probably small. But it could lead to some nasty surprises when the alternatives are more important or have non-obvious consequences.

◆   ◆   ◆

The idea that choice is a defining condition of freedom is not new. Among the authors who have explicitly mentioned this condition are Hume, Dewey, Laski, Fuller, Berlin, and Forbes. In the words of John Locke: "the idea of *liberty* is the idea of a power in any agent to do or forbear any particular action, according to the determination or thought of the mind, whereby either of them is preferred to the other.

But have I really *proved* that choice is a necessary condition of freedom? No. The issue of proof of the kinds of claims we are discussing now is a complicated one; and for that reason, I reserve a whole chapter for it later. What I am doing now is to illustrate the need for the condition and to show that the condition does apply to the kind of thing we are talking about when we talk of freedom.

To test whether any one of the conditions I will be proposing is really relevant to freedom or not, I'll be constructing contrasting situations that differ from each other only in that one situation *has* that condition and the other *lacks* it, or one situation has it to a greater extent than the other. The test then will be whether the difference in the situations makes a difference as to *how free* the person is in the two situations.

To carry out this test, each of us in reading the description of the situation will be asking ourselves whether we would feel more free in the one situation than in the contrasting situation. But does this tell us what we want to know? We are trying to get at *actual* freedom here, not merely *perceived* freedom. We want to know whether Mary really *is* more free, not whether she *thinks* she is more free.

But what is important here is that if we perceive a condition to make us feel more free or less so, that condition does fall within the connotation of the ordinary word "freedom." We can agree that we are not talking of cabbages or kings. What we are saying does apply to the *sort of thing* we mean when we use our word "freedom."

The justification will be carried out later.

◆   ◆   ◆

Note: Feeling free and being free

Of course, if a person feels less free in one situation than in another, then that person *is* less free in a sense. For example, if Mary feels oppressed, she is less free than she would be if she did not feel oppressed. That a person *feels* less free in situation **A** than in situation **B** does *not* imply that the person *is* less free when the feeling is based on differences in or accuracy of information in **B**. In general, *feeling free* does *not* imply *being free* because of the possibility of misinformation or deception. The examples used in the text, however, assume that the information level is the same in the two contrasted situations. So, the *feeling* of being more free or less so in the two contrasted situations *can* be used as a touchstone of the relevance of the condition which forms the basis of the contrast.

◆   ◆   ◆

All right, let's complicate the first situation. Suppose Mary must keep standing motionless, but the white seamless paper behind her (which she cannot see or feel) can be either one millimeter thick or two. And suppose she is allowed to make one choice and that is to choose the thickness of the paper. Now, she has a choice. Is she free?

We've agreed that choice is a *necessary* condition of freedom and we've given the person in this situation a choice. Can we now say that she is free? (In other words, we are now asking whether choice is also a *sufficient* condition of freedom.)

Strange as it may seem, there are quite respectable political theorists who would answer this question with a "yes:" Mary is now free.

Yet, any prisoner in the most tightly controlled prison would be as free as the proverbial bird by comparison with Mary. People in the most heinous dictatorial regimes would rejoice to stay where they are rather than be put in the situation Mary is in. And yet Mary is free?

◆　　◆　　◆

Note: worthless "freedom"

There are theorists who would try to get out of situations like this by answering: "Yes, the person is free, but her freedom is worthless to her." But our goal here is *not* to define a concept of freedom such that freedom is worthless. We are trying to define freedom in such a way that it can be a goal of public policy.

◆　　◆　　◆

If you've read the previous chapter, you might try a sophisticated counter-argument by saying, "Well, isn't the person free a little? Doesn't Mary have a tiny, infinitesimal degree of freedom?"

The answer is no. We are assuming that the person in this situation does not *care* what the thickness of the paper is. She is able to choose, but only about something that doesn't make any difference to her. If she could choose the temperature of the room, or whether the air is clean or dirty, or how much light there is in the room, or something else she cares about, we could say that she had some tiny degree of freedom. But to be able to choose in a matter that makes no difference whatever to the person choosing (the decision-maker) is not to be free at all.

Try a different situation. You are in a room, and the only thing you are aware of, the only thing you can see is a television screen, and the only thing you can do is to choose to watch channel **A** or channel **B**. Now, suppose both channels are showing the same program. The reception is equally good on both channels, the quality of the picture and sound is the same. Are you free?

The point is this: choices that make absolutely no difference do not raise your level of freedom at all. The choices, the differences, have to be something you care about.

Now, let's complicate the situation still further. Suppose you have two options: you can have your arm pinched or you can have your toe-nails pulled out one by one. Your choice.

Now the two alternatives certainly make a difference to you. You definitely care which happens. You care a lot. Well then, are you now free?

I know you're thinking, "If this is freedom, who needs it?" But wait a bit. Let's not assume that it *is* freedom.

You are allowed to make the choice. But what kind of choice is this? What we are demanding when we fight for "freedom" is to be able to do what we want. And we do not want to be pinched, nor do we want our toenails pulled out. In other words, what we do want is not available in this situation. And it won't do to try to say we're free a little bit either. We don't want either of these alternatives *at all!* In the words of John Stuart Mill: "Liberty consists in doing what one desires."

◆   ◆   ◆

Note: descriptive linguistics?

Have we departed from the connotations of the ordinary English word "freedom" in ruling out such a choice? It is debatable whether we have. Choice is one of the connotations. Doing what we want is another connotation. But what we are trying to do here is not an exercise in descriptive linguistics. We are not trying to come up with a definition of freedom that will be a complete and accurate reflection of all the connotations of the ordinary word "freedom." Even if we did, some of these connotations would be inconsistent with others. What we are trying to do is come up with a concept of liberty that can serve as an ultimate goal of society. And situations in which people are forced to make Hobson's Choice are not what anyone would want as part of the society we should be striving to attain.

◆   ◆   ◆

First approximate definition of freedom

We are now in a position to state our first approximation to a complete definition of liberty: To be at all free in a particular situation, we must have a choice, and the options from which we can choose must contain at least one whose value to us reaches some level acceptable to us.

For example, we can watch a television program that we want to watch or we can not watch it. We can either watch one program we like or watch another we like.

◆   ◆   ◆

Note: only one option?

What if there is only one acceptable option? Do we really have a choice? Are we really free? To say this is to say that *not* doing it is unacceptable. This does indeed mean that we are compelled *to some degree*.

But what if not doing it is okay, but just barely. Are we free? This is a question that is of more importance theoretically than practically. As long as we have an acceptable option and we can do it or not, we are free *to some degree*.

Even when we do have more than one acceptable option, often it will be obvious which option is the *most* desirable one to us. Hence, our decision is again trivially easy. Still, this type of case bothers us: Isn't our choice a foregone conclusion? Yes it is, but this does not mean our freedom disappears in these cases. It is still we who make the choice, who make the decision, it is we who evaluate the alternatives and conclude that one is the one we like best.

The times when situations of this sort represent low levels of freedom or even absence of freedom is when the situation is rigged, when someone makes us an "offer we can't refuse." When someone else sets up the options in such a way as to force us to choose exactly one of the options, then we have been compelled. We deal with situations like this in a later chapter.

◆   ◆   ◆

But let's introduce a further complication: suppose the situation we are in contains an option that is acceptable to us, but it isn't the one that we "really" want to do: we really want to go skiing, not watch television.

We have to be careful how we phrase things here. To say that an option is "acceptable" to us is to say that we really want to do it. What we mean here is that there is another course of action (skiing) that is not available in this situation and *that* is what we most want to do. If this were a situation in which we were completely free, we would choose that option, we would go skiing.

Yet, it still seems reasonable to say that a person who can either watch a program he likes or not watch it is free.

We seem to be faced with a paradox. We detect a difference in these situations, and we are sure that the difference is one of freedom and not some other difference. Yet, we don't want to throw out the case of the television watching as "not free." What are we to do?

If you've read the first chapter, you will have guessed the answer by this time. These two situations differ in their *level of freedom*. We have a person who is not completely unfree: in both situations she can either watch television (something she likes to do) or not. But at the moment she cares more about skiing than watching television. Yet in one situation, she can't go skiing. In the other situation, she can. Moreover, it is the option she prefers that is not available in this situation.

Second approximate definition of freedom

As a second approximation to a complete definition of liberty, then, we can say: The higher the value to the person of the most valued option available in a given situation, the higher the person's *level of freedom* in that situation.

In the situations above, going skiing has a higher value for Mary than watching television; but in the first situation, going skiing is not available; in the second it is. Mary's level of freedom is higher in the second situation than in the first.

Of course, the situations that we have been considering have to be complicated considerably before we are dealing with anything approximating the real world. But we have made considerable progress in this short time: we now realize that two conditions that define freedom are having options that are of value to us and being able to choose between them.

Yet these two conditions, choice and value, are not as simple as they appear; and some of their complications we must deal with, if we are to understand freedom in the real world.

Value

The value of an option seems to be a simple matter: we either like to go skiing or we do not like it. But as soon as we think about it, it begins to be more complex. First of all, we like skiing to a certain extent, to a certain degree. We enjoy it more than watching television, but not as much as sailing, let's say.

Moreover, skiing is not a unitary or momentary experience, but an activity: We wait in line. The man behind us in line is blowing cigarette smoke on us. We ride up on the ski lift. The weather is sunny and dry or it is cloudy and misty. We wait in line. The woman behind us is making nasty remarks about the Democrats or about the Republicans. We ski down the slope. The snow is either fine and powdery or icy in patches. And so on. Some of these features of skiing we like, others we don't like. Yet, all of them taken together make up the activity of skiing.

In other words, we have mixed feelings about skiing. And this is typical of many, if not most, of the things in life we like.

Furthermore, the value of an activity can be a volatile thing. Even if the weather and snow are fine, we may not enjoy skiing on a given day as much as we thought we would. Consequently, there is always an element of uncertainty about the value of an activity or of an object.

And if we are going skiing the day after the break-up of a relationship or of a marriage, we may not enjoy skiing at all.

All of these factors complicate our problem of choosing our most valued option.

The situation we are in gets even more complicated if we look below the psychological surface (as we will in a later chapter). Some people have experienced a "let-down" feeling after doing something they thought they would enjoy and believed they *were* enjoying while they were doing it. Such experiences let us know that it is possible to *misperceive* the value of an activity. Some literary authors have gone to the extreme of claiming that all experiences of enjoyment or pleasure are self-deceptions: "Happiness is a perpetual possession of being well-deceived."

◆   ◆   ◆

Note: You just *think* you like it!
This cavalier writing off of human valuing is too hasty, however. It is possible to come up with cases in which Mary misperceives her own valuation of something, but such cases are not easy to come by. And

certainly, the universal generalization that every case of perceiving something to be valuable is a misperception has most of the evidence going against it at this point.

To discriminate between whether Bill really likes something or only "thinks" he likes it, both the outsider and Bill himself can look at his behavior. For example, Bill says, "I really like classical music." But does he ever listen to classical music? No. This behavior provides a clue that Bill is probably deceiving himself about his valuation of classical music.

◆   ◆   ◆

Choice

Choosing between two or more options looks like a simple matter, especially in the kinds of cases we have been considering: watch channel **A** or watch channel **B**, go skiing or not, etc. But quite a bit goes on each time we make a choice, and it happens regardless of the extent to which we are aware of it.

In choosing, we are weighing alternatives. That means, we are trying to decide which of the options has more value for us. Sometimes it is obvious, sometimes not. Sometimes it appears obvious and we find out afterwards we were mistaken.

To weigh alternatives, then, requires a certain amount of insight into yourself. The better you know yourself, the better you know what the value of an option is for you.

But in many situations, especially those in which we are aware that we are making a choice, the options we are choosing between are not activities we enjoy doing for themselves but are activities we predict will lead to a desired result.

For example, if a man says, "Paint my house and I'll give you a thousand dollars," we predict (and probably assume in this case) that he will actually give us the money when we've finished painting the house. The option that we are choosing in this one simple situation is *not* whether or not to paint the house. We are choosing whether to paint-the-house-and-get-a-thousand-dollars or not. Like skiing, this is an activity over time; but assuming we do not enjoy painting houses, this activity is unlike skiing in that the value of the option comes at the end of the activity and is not interspersed here and there along the way (between the waiting in line).

Obviously, it makes a great deal of difference whether the thousand dollars is actually forthcoming after we finish painting the house. We predict that it will be, but we do not know for sure. We say that we will "probably" get paid.

We call receiving the money a possible "consequence" of painting the house.

Definition

A **consequence** is a result which follows (with a certain probability) from a course of action.

The consequences we are concerned about, of course, are the ones that make a difference to us. They are benefits and harms. They are rewards and punishments. Such consequences have an impact on our level of freedom. If the thousand dollars is not forthcoming, painting the house is not the option we would have chosen. We chose to paint the house on the assumption that this consequence was part of the option. We could be mistaken.

Moreover, if we slip on the scaffolding and fall and break a leg, breaking a leg is also a consequence of the activity of painting the house. We do not know whether we will fall or not. We consider it unlikely. But since such a consequence is possible, it is part of the option that we are considering.

There are a number of possible consequences of any given option, then, some of which may be unknown to us, and each occurs with a certain probability. What these probabilities are is often unknown to us when we make our choice. What all this shows is that when we make decisions, we are taking, usually a smaller, but sometimes a greater risk.

We can ignore one or more possible consequences when we are choosing, we can refuse to think about them, but they are there nonetheless. If we embark on this activity, we may well get some of these consequences too. And if an event is an actual consequence of a course of action (and not just a possible consequence), we cannot do the action without experiencing the consequence. To choose that option is to get the action *and* its consequences.

Preliminary definition of "option"

Thus, we need to specify that by an **option** we mean an available course of action *and* its consequences.

Now, suppose we possess that most useful of science-fiction devices, a crystal ball. This crystal ball will provide us with all the relevant information that we will need in a given choice situation, and we are guaranteed that the information is accurate.

Suppose we are in the choice situation in which we are deciding whether or not to paint the house. We look into this crystal ball and see that three days after starting to paint the house, a patch of grease that the owner's young son spilled on the scaffolding will cause us to fall to the ground and break a leg. Our choice will now be different. We will choose not to paint the house.

In one version of this choice situation, we have a crystal ball; in the other, we don't have a crystal ball. The question is this: Are we equally free in the two choice situations?

At the moment of making the choice, we are equally well off. In one case, we are standing there trying to decide whether to take the painting job or not. In the other case, we are making the same decision, but we have a crystal ball tucked under one arm. At that moment, our level of welfare may be the same. But also at that moment, we sense that we are more free in the one case than in the other because a condition, relevant to freedom, is different in the two cases.

That difference, of course, is in our level of (relevant) *information*.

Improved definition of "choice"

By a **choice** we mean weighing the value to us of the available **options** and selecting the one with the highest value. Such weighing presupposes knowing what the **options** are.

Knowledge

If someone says, "Which do you choose, **A** or **B**?", we would say, "I don't know. Tell me what **A** and **B** are, and I'll tell you which I choose."

An "option" cannot increase Bill's freedom if Bill does not know about the option and know its value. "Whoever determines what alternatives shall be known to a man controls what that man shall choose from. He is deprived of freedom in proportion as he is denied access to any ideas, or is confined to any range of ideas short of the totality of relevant possibilities." A child locked in a room who does not *know how* to use the key is no less a prisoner than an adult who does not *have* the key. And a child who knows how to use the key is more free than one who does not.

Similarly, to choose a course of action without knowing the consequences would be equally absurd, because once we embark on a course of action, we are stuck with the consequences. Knowledge of the consequences is thus essential to freedom. Research indicates that some people regard situations in which the person knows the consequences of the alternatives as more free than situations in which such knowledge is unavailable. "The road to freedom may be found in that knowledge of facts which enables us to employ them in connection with desires and aims....Intelligence is the key to freedom in act."

But *amount* of information varies, as does its *reliability* and *validity*. And these factors affect the extent to which the information supports conclusions that are relevant to freedom. That is, conclusions that pertain to conditions that are relevant, such as the consequences of the actions and their value to us. Although Mary, who does not know that she has unreliable information, may *feel* as free as Jane, who has reliable information, it seems reasonable to say that she is not as free. Certainly, over time as the unreliability shows up in failure of things to function as they are believed to function, surprising or shocking consequences of apparently reasonable courses of action, and so forth, the low level of freedom becomes clear and begins to be perceived.

Bill, who has certain mistaken beliefs as to how an automobile works, cannot carry out a course of action that involves use of an automobile. And Mary, whose information as to how other people will react in various situations is unreliable, may have a course of action interrupted or see it produce unexpected results.

Bill, who draws invalid inferences from the information available, is in a similar situation; for, a statement invalidly derived from a true statement may or may not be true. Hence, Bill may find himself forced to make more decisions and new plans as the old ones fail to work. Of course, the most rational information-handling will not avoid problems of incomplete, only partially reliable information, but irrationality may exacerbate these problems. Hence, in at least some cases, a person who is able to handle information rationally is more free.

To sum up: the longer Mary's planning horizon and the more dependable her knowledge of her options, the more free she is, even in the present situation.

◆   ◆   ◆

Note: too much information?

Sometimes it is claimed that a person may be overwhelmed by the quantity of information available. Doesn't this decrease freedom? There are several possible cases here.

For one, Bill may be faced by stacks of books, papers, reports, documents, all of which contain information he needs in order to make a decision by tomorrow night. The problem here is that the information is in the books, not in Bill's head. Bill has, not too much, but too little information (in his head).

Second, Mary may have a great deal of information about the choice situation except for one or more key pieces of information and she may find decision-making difficult. The problem here is the missing information, not too much information.

Third, Bill may have all the information necessary for making a decision, but it may not be organized in such a way that it can be used and may be mixed up with a great deal of information that is not relevant to this particular decision. Bill simply cannot process the information to make the decision. The problem here is not too much information, but an organization that makes the information unusable.

Finally, Mary may not be willing to take the time to plough through her information, weigh it and make the decision. For trivial decisions, this is probably reasonable. But when important decisions come along, not having organized one's information ahead of time or being unwilling to search through it, turns out to be self-destructive.

I suspect that cases in which there is actually too much information are rare.

◆   ◆   ◆

People sometimes do what they want to do, not knowing the consequences, and get clobbered as a result. As we saw in the first chapter, this fact has been used as an argument against freedom. But people who do not know and do not bother to learn the consequences of their actions are already not very free when they are choosing. The remedy is to help them become more free, not to redefine or reject freedom.

Sometimes the consequences are difficult to determine, but this does not mean that freedom is a bad thing and that we are better off if someone else tells us what to do. It simply means that there are times in life when our level of freedom is low. We should work to make it higher, not give it away altogether.

Freedom across situations

Immediately after we are in a single situation, of course, we are in another situation. And we are as concerned with what our level of freedom is in that situation as we were in the first situation. Everything that has been said so far about freedom in a single situation applies, naturally, to the new situation.

What concerns us here, though, is that some of the consequences of our actions in the first situation may affect our level of freedom in the second situation. Which consequences are these? Any consequences which increase or decrease the availability of the options in this situation, or which increase or decrease their value, or which increase or decrease our knowledge of their value or availability. In other words, any consequences which affect one or more of the defining conditions of freedom.

Of course, other conditions may exist in the second situation which are not a consequence of our actions. If these conditions affect the availability or value of the options in that situation or our knowledge thereof, they affect our level of freedom. These conditions which can *affect* our level of freedom encompass a wide range of personal, interpersonal, economic, organizational, social, and political practices. I have devoted an entire chapter to a discussion of these conditions affecting freedom. Any public policies to improve our degree of freedom must operate on these conditions.

◆   ◆   ◆

Note: causation and freedom

Some people, especially literary people, believe that the fact that causes operate on human behavior means that freedom does not exist. Several types of cases are offered. Suppose Bill loves sailing more than anything in the world, and John says, "I've just rented a boat. Let's go sailing." It is held that John's statement "causes" Bill to go sailing. Therefore, Bill is not really free. But John's providing the opportunity to go sailing free of charge is not an interference with Bill's freedom. In fact, John has increased Bill's freedom. Similarly, seeing "his" slot machine gushing money at Reno "causes" Bill to reach for the money. This is not an interference with Bill's freedom, but an expression of it.

A slightly more sophisticated version of this argument holds that whatever caused Bill to love sailing in the first place has forever interfered with Bill's freedom, since for the rest of Bill's life, that value (love of sailing) will *force* Bill to go sailing whenever he gets a chance (especially if a free ride is offered by a friend). But having valued options is not an interference with freedom, it is necessary to freedom. The person who has nothing much that he likes to do is the one whose freedom is low.

By contrast, a poor child who is taught to have expensive tastes he can never satisfy will have a low level of freedom.

Another variation on this claim is the psychopathological one. People's choices are undermined by unconscious forces. This does indeed sometimes happen, and I can do no better than recommend psychotherapy. But literary people sometimes believe that all human behavior is undermined by such unconscious forces. There is no evidence to support such a sweeping generalization. The pathological cases stand out precisely because they are abnormal. Depth psychological factors are discussed in more detail in a later chapter.

◆   ◆   ◆

Delayed consequences

Some of the consequences of our actions may not be felt in the immediately following situation, but in a much later situation. For example, if in the first situation I eat a large meal and am satiated, the fact that I ate the last remaining food I have or will ever have may not affect my level of freedom in the second situation. But eventually as the days pass without food, I will be in a situation in which it *will* affect my level of freedom.

Other consequences may not be felt immediately because they are part of a causal chain, that is, one consequence causes another consequence which does not affect me but causes another consequence which does affect me. For example, if in the first situation I insult someone, and that person plots to kill me next year, I have affected my level of freedom in some situation next year. (The influence of other people on one's level of freedom is discussed in chapters 3 and 6.)

Creation of options: goals

Of course, we may be able to undertake courses of action in the first situation that create or make available additional options in the second situation. For example, if Mary wants to study painting in a community that has no art school, she might be able to get together an art club and hire a teacher. Similarly, Bill by learning more about something may learn to value it, thus providing himself with another possible alternative.

These courses of action in the first situation that create options in the second *may* themselves be ones we like to do, but often they are not. Often in fact they are rather unpleasant.

When we look at our level of freedom in the first and second situations combined, then, we have to look not only at the value of the option in the second situation, but at the value (low or negative) of the option that we chose in the first situation in order to create that option in the second situation.

Costs of an option

We can call these less valued tasks that we undertake to make available an option **A,** the *costs* of **A**. The cost of an action is a function of such things as the difficulty of the task, its unpleasantness, and the adequacy of the time available for carrying out the task.

◆   ◆   ◆

We must also consider the possibility that the tasks that we perform may not succeed in making available the option **A**. One strategy, of course, is to try not to acquire tastes that are costly or difficult to make available.

Equal value and flexibility

Sometimes more than one option has equal value as far as we are concerned. And sometimes this is true of the highest priority option. When we have several options which have the highest value for us, our level of freedom is much more likely to be high. Why? If one of these options is not available, another one may be. In other words, we have flexibility we would not have if we had only one option we valued as highest.

Similarly, a person whose second-highest valued option is far less valued that the highest valued option is in a much more vulnerable position. If the preferred option is not available, the person has very little to fall back on. In general, the "distance" between the most desired option and the most desired *available* option is one measure of how free we are. People who cannot gain admittance to a career they prefer will be more free if there is another career open that they would also like very much than they would be if the only other alternatives were mildly interesting to them.

Satisfaction and the rotation of priorities

Another feature of the way humans value things is the fact of satisfaction. What happens in satisfaction is that the value of an option decreases temporarily. For example, if I am very hungry, eating is my most valued option. But as soon as I have eaten, eating is not very high on my list of things to do. Obviously, hunger is a value which increases "automatically" or by itself over a period of time, so that eventually it will be the highest priority option again.

Another obvious example of this rotation of priorities is sex. But all human values follow this pattern. With satisfaction, their value decreases more or less, but eventually their value will again be high enough that we will choose that option over others.

Some values take longer to reach satiation, decrease in value only slightly and bounce back quickly: writing a philosophy paper, for example. (Just kidding!) Other options are satisfied more quickly and take longer to reach a value high enough that we choose them: attending a party, for example. (Obviously, these examples are matters of taste and vary widely between individuals.)

So, even in those short periods of time when we are completely free, we do not eat all the time, nor have sex all the time, nor even write philosophy papers all the time. We vary our activities.

Other kinds of options

We have been talking of options as courses of action. It is now time to make clear that what has been said need not be restricted to actions. Since we value more than just actions in our lives, the concept of freedom must refer to other things as well. We want not just to *do* things, but we want to *be* in situations or have environmental conditions we like, we want to *feel* whatever we enjoy feeling (and not be subjected to unpleasant feelings against our wills), and we want to be able to *think* freely.

Final definition of options

An **option**, then, is any available course of action, feeling, situation or thought and its consequences and our level of information thereof.

Final definition of freedom or liberty

Our **level of freedom** is the "composite" of the values of the (available) options which have the highest priority in each succeeding situation of our lives. (Remember that "option" includes the completeness and degree of probability of the relevant information we have and our ability to process that information.)

What does "composite value" mean? The composite value of the first situation and the second situation is the value for us of the two situations taken together. Even an activity like going skiing is a composite value made up of many positive and negative experiences. The same may be said of all the successive situations that make up our lives.

This is not to say that combining the values of courses of action and of consequences is an easy judgment to make, nor that we might not be mistaken in making it. But such a judgment does have meaning. If we could live a portion of our lives twice, experiencing first one series of situations and then the other series, we could pick the one we prefer. In actual fact, we try in our imaginations to do just that when we are attempting to weigh two alternatives. How far we look ahead depends on our knowledge of the consequences of the options and how important we think those consequences will be.

Freedom is thus defined over the lifetime of the individual person.

If Mary has a high level of freedom in one situation and no freedom at all for the rest of her life, she is not very free. Mary is free *to the extent* that she can do, be, think or feel whatever she wants whenever she wants throughout her life.

Limiting Freedom

We have seen that it is better to talk about degrees of freedom than about whether someone is simply free or not free. This allows us to ask the question whether people *should be* as free as possible, in other words whether the ultimate goal of a society should be to *maximize* individual freedom.

As noted in the first chapter, the attitude of most people varies on this question: When it is *my* freedom we're talking about, I should definitely be as free as possible; when it is *your* freedom, then I'm not so sure.

But let's approach the question a different way: Why should people *not* be as free as possible?

One of the problems about freedom that worried theorists in the past was that people sometimes use their freedom to do things they later regret having done. This was used as an argument that freedom is not necessarily a good thing. But because of the way freedom has been defined in the previous chapter, we have eliminated this problem. We have seen that when you have to act without knowing the full consequences of what you propose to do (or to act while under a mistaken impression about what the consequences will be), you are not as free as you otherwise would be. If you had known what those consequences would be, you would have been more free. So, if you are as free as possible, you know what the consequences would be of what you want to do, and thus would not choose to hurt yourself.

So, this problem no longer provides a reason for limiting the freedom of people. What other reasons might there be?

Like most people, what worries me when thinking of the freedom of other people is the distinct possibility that those other people might use their freedom to hurt me or to interfere with what I want to do. And most people would agree with limiting the other person's liberty in cases like this.

At first glance, it appears that we have a conflict between liberty and harm; and it is tempting to go on to raise the question: which is more important, liberty or harm? But it is not necessary to create this problem. There is another way to ask the same question.

If I am harmed, I am obviously experiencing something I do not want to experience. If freedom is experiencing what you want to experience, then my freedom has been interfered with here. In other words, my liberty has been limited.

What we have in this situation, then, is not a question whether (anyone's) freedom should be limited, but *whose* freedom should be limited, mine or the other person creating the harm.

◆   ◆   ◆

Another argument, heard more often in the past than today but still around, is the claim that a person should not be at liberty to do something *immoral*. This argument appears plausible, and it sets up a dilemma between liberty and morality: which has priority?

But as one begins to look at this dilemma, the first thing that becomes clear is that the problem, apparently rather simple as stated, is complicated. Whose morality are we going to use to decide cases involving a conflict between liberty and morality, mine or yours? The proponents must justify their claim that *their* version of morality is better than everyone else's version. Otherwise, their rules are simply the opinions of the person stating them; and while we might respect their right to their opinion, we see no reason why we and other people should be bound by them. The problem, thus, has gone from being merely complicated, to being very difficult.

Attempts to justify a set of moral rules have been based on the claim that they were for the acting person's own good or have appealed to the advisability not to harm other people, both of which proposed criteria we have shown to be encompassed by the theory of freedom presented here. Consequently, we are back to the problem of whose liberty to limit.

But stepping back from this morass of problems for a moment, we might wonder: why *would* someone want to do something that was immoral? What's in it for them? In the past, this question was easy to answer. Many of life's greatest joys, such as having sex, were ruled out as immoral. This situation led to such one-liners as: "If it feels good, it's probably bad." The moralists who propounded these rules in the distant past undoubtedly had their own motives for being upset that other people were having sex; but more recently such rules have given morality itself a bad name, and most recent moralists have quietly dropped them.

So, the question remains: why *would* someone want to do something immoral? Attempts to answer this question tend to come again and again to examples in which what one person wants to do harms someone else or interferes with what someone else wants to do.

Since under the theory of freedom presented here, harm is itself a limit on the harmed person's freedom, the grounds being appealed to for limiting an acting person's liberty is that not limiting it would result in limiting the harmed person's liberty. In other words, using the present definition of freedom, conflict between the freedoms of different people is the only grounds needed for limiting the freedom of any one person. Thus, we do not need a value, ranking higher than freedom, for deciding whether or not to limit freedom. Freedom itself provides the criterion.

Of course, the theory of liberty that I am presenting here must be subjected to the same requirement as other views: it must be justified. And this task I address in a later chapter. To the extent that my justification is correct, attempts to find other criteria than liberty for limiting freedom are not only unjustified but unjustifiable. One of the most formidable other criteria is the concept of justice. And it is to the concept of justice I turn in the next chapter.

Conflict of liberties

This still leaves a host of difficult practical and theoretical problems concerning exactly how or when or on what grounds to limit an individual's freedom. In order to deal with these problems, we need to classify conflicts into types. These types can be any types we like. The task is to construct the classes in such a way as to enable us to find resolutions for conflicts of that type.

First, let's recognize a type that provides no real problem of conflict resolution. Suppose Jones wants to tell Smith what to do. Smith does not want to be told what to do. We have a conflict between Jones and Smith. How do we resolve it?

This one is easy. And the decision would of course go against Jones. Why? Because there is no way Jones can justify controlling Smith's behavior. Jones could claim to be in possession of the one right morality. But lacking a justification for that claim, Jones has no justification for controlling Smith; and Jones's freedom, his attempt to control Smith, will be the one that is limited in this case.

Scarcity-based conflicts

Let's begin with an example. Suppose Judy and Mary want to use an astronomical telescope tonight. But suppose further that there is only one such telescope available to them.

Here we have a conflict between what Judy wants to do and what Mary wants to do. They cannot both use the same telescope at the same time. Either Judy's freedom will be limited or Mary's will be. The problem is: whose liberty should be limited?

This example is paradigmatic of the type of conflict I shall call "scarcity-based." There is nothing wrong with Judy wanting to use the telescope, and there is nothing wrong with Mary wanting to use it. Judy does not object in principle to Mary's using the telescope, and Mary does not object to Judy's using it. The only reason they are in conflict is that there aren't enough telescopes to go around. In other words, the basis for this conflict is the scarcity of telescopes.

A large number of the conflicts familiar in our everyday lives are scarcity-based conflicts. Obvious examples are uses of all "public" or "collective" goods. There are only so many slots available at a public picnic area. There are only so many square inches available on a public beach. There are only so many public tennis courts, only so many cubic feet available in a public swimming pool, etc.

Less obvious examples are: amount of space available on the roads and highways, public sidewalks, subways and buses, parks, etc.

◆　　　◆　　　◆

We have rules and conventions for the resolution of these conflicts: for example, the rule known as "first come first served" or FIFO. But are these rules and conventions right? Are they the best way to resolve these conflicts of liberties?

It is important to recognize (as you do if you are in such a conflict and the decision goes against you) that such methods do not really solve anything. This is one reason the word "resolve" is used. The person who packs a picnic basket, packs the kids and drives all the way across town to have a picnic and then finds all the space taken has had her freedom arbitrarily limited, even if she agrees with the FIFO rule.

It is not like the "rule of the road." You are no worse off if everyone drives on the right side of the road than if everyone drives on the left. It is simply a rule that resolves and prevents lots of conflicts. But FIFO does not do that. In FIFO, if you get there second, you cannot do what you wanted to do. Period.

Much effort and ink has been expended trying to make people feel that somehow rules like FIFO make everything all right, and that to believe that somehow things are not as good as they could be is immature, irrational, or whatever. There are even elaborate attempts to make a case that the situation is "just": for example, that you have an equal chance to get there first. Or even, that it is your own fault (or better still, your wife's fault): if you had left sooner, you would have gotten there first.

(I would conjecture that most if not all traditional moral rules are attempts, like this one, not to solve the problem of legitimate conflicts, but to avoid the problem. I further suspect that much that happens in marriage counseling sessions may fall into the same category. And the results are the same. People who follow the moral prescriptions or the counseling advice sometimes have an unsettling, unsatisfied feeling, the way a person who plays a game of cards sometimes feels that somehow, somewhere, he has been cheated.)

But not everyone is convinced by any one of these methods of resolution. In fact, so much disagreement has centered around every method of conflict resolution that has ever been proposed that some people have wondered whether some conflicts are not impossible in principle to resolve. Others have suspected that there is some fundamental problem, some philosophical or value-based problem, underlying these conflicts which has yet to be clarified and resolved.

Ultimate goals and intermediate goals

My method of attacking this problem is two-fold: first, let's see if we can agree on what *would be* a resolution if we were able to put it into practice. Let's set aside for the moment questions of feasibility, of present technology, of economic costs, etc. Of course, if we can prove that a proposed solution cannot in principle be implemented, that it is not simply a question of our present technology or resources, then we will have to rule out that proposed solution. A solution we can never put into practice is useless to us.

Second, let's formulate a development path that will lead in the direction of that solution, approaching closer and closer.

This gives us not only a solution but a path toward that solution. Public policy as well as individual morality then would have a criterion to guide them: policies would be justified to the extent that they moved society forward along this path, and the preferred policies would be those that moved us along farthest or fastest.

Solution

What, then, is the solution to scarcity-based conflicts? The solution, the ultimate goal of society, is (surprisingly enough) to eliminate the scarcity on which these conflicts are based.

Implementation

Fine, but how do we implement such a theory? How do we approach this utopian condition?

Short of miraculous technological developments such as nuclear fusion or quick and inexpensive shuttles to some other planet where we can transplant half our population, one path is to increase *per capita* goods, services, and resources. That means, increase what each person has.

To do this, two steps are necessary, and they are both obvious:

One: increase production of goods and/or services. Theoretically, it would be nice to increase resources too, but this is not possible.

Second: reduce population size. If there are fewer people and the same or more goods, then the amount of goods per person increases.

I'll discuss later the formidable problems of implementing the second part of this plan. But it must be said here that, obviously, no one is proposing reducing population by going around and shooting people or by sterilizing them or by any other heinous method. More surprisingly, perhaps, it is not even necessary to take away each person's privilege of having a child. (Ridiculous! Most people would say. How can you reduce population size if every man and woman on the planet has a child?) Simple. It takes *two*, one man and one woman, to have *one* child. Let that suffice for now. The problems that remain are formidable, probably in practice insurmountable, but they are political and religious problems, not philosophical or moral ones.

Interim resolutions

Concurrently with approaching a true solution to the problem by reducing scarcity, some resolutions are needed, painful though they may be. One if FIFO, already discussed above.

Another is the age-old resolution known on every playground as "taking turns." If you had the tennis court yesterday, I should have it today, even if you did get there one minute ahead of me.

This resolution has the advantage of "time-sharing" the scarce resource, so that everyone can do what he wants to do *some of the time*. It also avoids the panic associated with FIFO: you do not have to rush around, scream at the kids, etc. in order to use the scarce resource.

Another possible resolution, appropriate for some scarce resources, might be social benefit. To construct an obvious example, simply for purposes of illustrating the point: if a medical scientist wants to use a microscope and his junior-high-school son wants to use it, there might be more social benefit if the medical researcher used it. (Junior-high-school pupils will disagree, of course.)

Value-based conflicts

Obviously, not all conflicts are of this type. Consider the following case: You are sitting in a city park, quietly listening to the birds sing and contemplating the beauty of nature, when all at once the ground begins to shake, the trees vibrate, the birds scram and you are treated to the strains of someone's boom box a hundred yards away.

There is a conflict. What you want to do is sit in the park, enjoy peace and quiet and listen to the birds; what he wants to do is sit in the park and listen to The Doors. If you are to do what you want to do, he has to turn it off. But that would mean that he cannot do what he wants to do.

The basis for this conflict is a difference in values. He likes The Doors, you like the birds. If everyone in the park at that time valued the birds, or alternatively valued The Doors, there would be no conflict and no one's freedom would have to be limited. It will do no good to argue which is better, the birds or The Doors. You will never convince him, just as he will never convince you.

There are many examples of conflicts of this type. The two people in question might not be sitting in a city park. Jones might be sitting in his living room reading. Smith might be sitting in his living room, listening to the Grateful Dead. Jones would be grateful if Smith were dead. But unfortunately, they are sitting in their separate living rooms, two feet apart, with only two half-inch pieces of sheet rock between them.

Mary might be a smoker, Judith a non-smoker, sitting at separate tables at a restaurant.

Much effort has been expended trying to decide whose freedom should be limited in cases like these. Neither side is necessarily doing anything wrong. Neither party wants his/her liberty limited.

Value-based conflicts due to scarcity

My first observation about this class of conflicts is that theoretically they are based on scarcity. The conflicts could be totally eliminated without limiting the freedom of either party if there were more of something or other.

If there were thicker walls and sound-proofing, Smith could listen to the Grateful Dead and still be friends with Jones. If there were sufficient ventilation systems, plastic partitions, etc. both Mary and Judith could eat at the same restaurant without hating each other. If there were enough space so that some parks could have a "party" atmosphere, while other parks were reserved for peace and quiet, both the birds and The Doors could co-exist.

The ultimate solution to these conflicts then, is the same as for scarcity-based conflict: more resources and smaller population. But what interim solutions are available?

Interim solutions

First, we can say that if one of the parties to the conflict has another place where he can do the same thing he is doing now, he should go to that place. This would completely eliminate the conflict, although at some inconvenience to one of the people.

Another criterion used to resolve such conflicts involves arranging harms into a hierarchy, such as physiological harms, psychological harms, and matters of taste. If what one person wants to do is merely a matter of taste, yet it is having the effect of physiologically damaging another person, then it should be the freedom of the former person which is limited. For example, if Jones thinks it might be fun to stick a knife into Smith, Jones's freedom to do so should be limited. This criterion may appear intuitive enough, maybe even obvious. But consider another case. Jones thinks it might be enjoyable to smoke in a room with Smith. Is the criterion still obvious?

Beyond this, the criteria that have been proposed become more debatable. One example is the criterion that dislikes should outweigh likes. If Jones wants to play folk music on the radio, and Smith does not want to hear it, Smith's dislike should outweigh Jones' liking. The rationale here is that it is easier to give up something one wants than to be subjected to something one finds disagreeable. Jones can find something else to do; and even if he can't, he is not going to suffer. Smith, on the other hand, would actually be suffering.

One might be tempted to propose that the intensity of the wants should be taken into account. In extreme cases this might be possible: Jones finds it pleasant to have a television going in the background even though he isn't watching it or even consciously listening to it; Smith goes bananas every time a commercial comes on. In many cases, though, it is not possible to compare the intensity of one person's valuation with the intensity of another person's.

Another proposed criterion is FIFO. Whoever got to the park first, The Doors or the birds, wins. The FIFO criterion has the same disadvantages here as before.

Another criterion is that the acting person, the one who is doing whatever it is that makes the conflict reveal itself, should be the one whose freedom is curtailed, in other words, the actor rather than the recipient of the act. (Notice that the actor does not *cause* the conflict. The conflict is caused by both the actor's values and the recipient's values.) The rationale for limiting the actor rather than the recipient is that the actor has more control over the situation. For example, if the case were decided by a coin toss, the actor could bring about a call for another coin-toss anytime he wanted to, simply by turning on the radio again or doing whatever it is that bothers the other person.

This criterion would yield exactly the same results as the "dislikes outweigh likes" criterion, yet the rationale is different here, since the actor has some control over the situation and can choose. The recipient cannot choose to abruptly switch what he dislikes.

One criterion which should never be used, but which sometimes is and which it would be easy to fall into, is majority rule. If a majority want the radio on, the radio stays on; if a majority want it quiet, it stays quiet. The rationale, obviously, is to try to satisfy as many people as possible. But under this criterion the freedom of the minority counts for nothing. Their freedom to have the condition they want in this case never prevails; the freedom of the majority always prevails. Contrast this with the time-sharing resolution above in which every individual can have what he wants some of the time. Also, use of this criterion fuels a population race, in which every group tries to become a majority.

Value-based conflicts in relationships

One thing that the examples used so far have in common is that the parties to the conflict are strangers. And the solution has been, in effect, to separate them either in time or as to place. Many value-based conflicts, however, occur between people who like each other and want to spend time together.

Julie wants to go out tonight; Ralph wants to stay home. John likes a house neat; wife Marsha likes it "homey." Linda is a compulsive house-cleaner; Charley likes to clean house once a month (whether it needs it or not).

Some of these conflicts are based on "head-on" differences in values: John likes it, Mary doesn't. Other conflicts of this type are based on differences in timing: Mary wants to do it now, John wants to do it some other time. Still other conflicts of this type are based on differences in priorities: although they both like baseball and opera, John would rather go to the baseball game than the opera, Mary would rather go to the opera than the baseball game.

The ultimate goal, the solution, in these cases cannot be to separate the two people. That is not what they want. These value-based conflicts are based also on some relationship or other between the persons involved in the conflict. In other words, these conflicts between John and Mary involve also an "internal conflict" within John and within Mary. Mary wants to go to the opera, but she also wants to be with John (and wants John to be enjoying himself while she is with him).

What is the solution? And what are the interim resolutions?

Solution

Since these conflicts are based on differences in values, the ultimate goal would seem to be to eliminate these differences.

But it has been argued that some people find the differences interesting. Some people even find them exciting. If we eliminate the differences between people in values and interests, won't they be bored with each other?

This is undoubtedly a theoretical argument, since it is probably impossible ever to eliminate all differences between people in both values, priorities, and even timing. But theory (more correctly, the ultimate goal toward which we should be working) is what we are concerned with at this point. Would it be a good thing if we *could* do it?

Certainly, surprise is a basis for interest. And when John and Mary find themselves at odds, they are at first surprised. And if they knew they would always agree, their futures would to a degree be quite predictable. On the other hand, if this surprise is too great, we call it a shock. Mary tells John, after ten years of marriage, that she has never found their sex life very exciting. This kind of surprise John doesn't need; neither does Mary.

Since mild surprises and occasional unpredictability are valued (let us say) by John and Mary, these values will have to be "traded off" with their values of going to the opera, the ball game, or whatever. The real situation, then, is that John values the ball game and also values occasional surprises. This is what he wants in his life. To eliminate these would not be what he wants. In other words, to eliminate these would render him less free than he would be if these elements were in his life.

We have here another conflict between some of John's own values, another internal conflict. Internal conflicts of this sort mean that some of John's values are incompatible with others of his values. If these incompatibilities are minor, do we have a problem here? What everyone, I think, will agree is that these conflicts need to be reduced far, far below where they are today for most of us.

We also have to be careful with the examples we have been using. All of them have involved only two people, John and Mary. In fact, people have several friends to whom they feel some degree of closeness and with whom they spend some of their time. The relevance of this fact is that this feature of human life provides a possible way of resolving the types of conflicts we are now considering.

One way for Mary to avoid the conflict with John over going to the ballgame and at the same time to go to the opera with someone she wants to go with is for Mary to go to the opera with Susan. This might work well if John can go to the ballgame with Bill. (We are all aware of the scheduling problems created by such solutions, as the telephone tag and the elaborate scheduling diaries kept by some people show.)

On this basis, then, we can state the following as the ultimate goal:

To reduce as far as possible the frequency and intensity of conflicts between persons involved in relationships with each other. But how?

Implementation

One method of approaching the ultimate goal may be called **substitutability**:

For any given value that a person has, there are **n** (0 or more) other people whom she likes who also have that value. The more other people for whom this is true and the more of a person's values for which this is true, the easier it will be for the person to eliminate the conflict.

Unfortunately, as these factors increase, the difficulty of scheduling also increases. But this is a technological problem and could easily be handled by "intelligent" answering machines (of the sort coming to be used in advanced office automation systems).

We must also be careful not to regard the status quo at any one time in our own society as an indication of what is possible or what can be desired by human beings. Lifestyles with regard to the factors we are now considering have been changing over the last two decades, more so in certain large cities than elsewhere.

◆   ◆   ◆

To evaluate this method of solving this type of conflict problem, we need answers to some factual questions:

(1) To what extent is it possible for a given human being to feel close to more than one other human being? We know that it is possible to be friends with more than one person at a time. How close can these friendships be? Is it possible to have strong feelings of caring for more than one person at a time? Are these feelings jeopardized if people have physical contact, for example, if they have sex with each other?

(2) To what extent is it possible to feel close to a person and at the same time be indifferent to whether this person feels close to other people as well? Does this feeling of indifference change if the other person touches or has sex with another person? In other words, to what extent are intimacy and possessiveness related? What implications, if any, does this double attitude of intimacy and indifference have for the future dependability of the relationship?

And for all of these questions, how much individual variation is there between people?

Answers to these questions are scarce. Anecdotal evidence indicates that persons who have sexual relationships with more than one person maintain a certain distance to each person, in other words, that the level of intimacy is not high. But this could be explained by other personality factors or it could reflect the fact that not many people are now involved in these "open" lifestyles, so the dependability of the lifestyle in the future is constantly in danger. Eliminating the option of sex could reduce these problems, but there would still be the fear of the possibility that sex might occur between the person one cares about and another person.

◆   ◆   ◆

Another long-term method of approaching the ultimate goal is to try to raise children in such a way as to minimize certain personal characteristics that increase the frequency and intensity of value-based conflicts.

One such characteristic is the number of *dislikes* a person has. The more dislikes a person has the more conflicts they are likely to experience and the more serious these conflicts will be. To take an extreme example: the neo-Hippie lifestyle attempts to accept almost any behavior of other people. The goal here is imperviousness, not to let anything bother one. This fits in well with the "anything goes" lifestyle. The problems are that there is a certain amount of self-deception involved in not letting anything bother one, and that there is unconscious group pressure to not recognize that one is bothered, especially since the official group ideology prescribes this.

Still, it is an open question how people in childhood acquire the dislikes they have and whether they *have to* acquire them. Also, the intensity of these dislikes varies between people, suggesting that a human being need not acquire intense dislikes. In addition, the dislikes of some people are attached to (what are to other people) extremely minute phenomena. The spoiled little rich girls of the fictional past are examples.

At the same time, great composers and poets and such have often been extremely "sensitive" people who responded strongly to stimuli which to other people were mild or even non-existent. Whether it would be good for society to weed out this sensitivity is therefore arguable.

◆   ◆   ◆

Second, the fewer *equivalences* there are in a person's value hierarchy and the greater the *distance* between ranks in that hierarchy, the more conflicts he will have and the more serious those conflicts will be.

If John likes opera equally as much as going to the ballgame, then the conflict between John and Mary is easily resolved: John can go to the opera with Mary. Resolution would also be easy if John likes the ballgame only a little better than the opera, since his desire to be with Mary would outweigh the difference. But if John likes the ballgame far better than the opera, then John's giving in would come at a price (for John and probably for Mary as well).

Also, some people are very *definite* (in other words, inflexible) about what they want to do at a particular time, while other people may often have only vague feelings.

And finally, some people have only a very *few values* in their hierarchies. They like to ride horses. Period. Unless they can find a partner with an equally impoverished value structure, they will often be in conflict with other people.

◆   ◆   ◆

Third, the more *intensely* the values are held, the more intense the conflict will be and the more difficult to resolve. If John hates folk dancing, and Mary wants to go folk dancing four nights a week, they have a problem.

◆   ◆   ◆

Fourth, the more inflexible people are with regard to *when* they do something, the more conflicts they will have. A person who must do something as soon as the idea hits him is in effect a person with only one value, while people who have a number of values and are happy when they can satisfy each these values within a few days have an easier time finding activities that do not conflict with what their friend wants to do. A person who is unable to delay gratification at all will be a difficult person to live with.

◆   ◆   ◆

Still, there may be cases where one or both of the parties will be more free if they end their relationship and find someone else.

One factor which affects that decision will be the seriousness of the conflicts between them. Seriousness is a function of the intensity of the values which are in conflict and the amount of time occupied by the value in conflict. For example, if John goes into withdrawal symptoms anytime rock music is not playing at full throttle, and Mary throws up every time she hears rock music, the two are probably not meant for each other, however many other values they have in common.

But even if the value in conflict is not very important to either of them, if it occurs all the time, it could be fatal to their relationship. For example, if Mary is a chain smoker and John is an anti-smoker, even if smoking is not very important to Mary, the two are probably not going to find their time together very enjoyable.

Other characteristics that are relevant are degree of hostility: some people seem to be more hostile in general toward other people than average. Another characteristic is considerateness: to take into account the effects of one's actions on other people as well as their effects on oneself could prevent many unintended conflicts.

Interim resolutions

Other than trying to develop extensive friendship networks and raise children in such a way as to minimize the development of the personal characteristics that increase conflict, what criteria can be used to resolve the conflicts that do occur between people who care about each other?

Certainly, the *hierarchy of harms* criterion discussed before could be and would be used by people in a relationship to decide whose freedom is to be limited.

And probably the criterion of *dislikes outweighing likes* would be used.

In addition, wise couples will probably try to compare the intensity of their values and resolve their conflict accordingly.

Serious or intense conflicts will probably be resolved by simply engaging in the activity with someone else rather than requiring one's partner to give in.

For milder conflicts involving scheduling or differences between two things both parties like to do, taking turns may be used.

Some values may be such that they cannot be delayed very long. For example, one person may need to go to the bathroom, the other person may not want to stop the car. These "fixed" values should take precedence over other values that can be delayed.

Some values people have are long-term values, others are short-term. If Mary is working to finish writing a book and John wants to go to a movie again tonight, Mary's value should take precedence. (Of course, John could go alone or with someone else, as discussed above.)

For additional arguments of more interest to philosophers and political theorists, see the Appendix: "For Professional Philosophers".

Freedom and Justice

Why a chapter on justice in a book on freedom?

Political theorists have long assumed that one of the goals of a society is to achieve justice. "Liberty and justice for all" is a slogan built into the pledge of allegiance to the U. S. flag.

Unfortunately, there appears to be a conflict between freedom and justice: If we maximize freedom, then the distribution of goods that results from people exercising their freedom in getting jobs, earning money, and so on, may or may not (but probably will not) conform to any theory of distributive justice; whereas, if we enforce a particular distribution of goods, then we must limit the freedom of individuals in order to do so, otherwise some people on their own initiative might get a larger share of goods than the theory of justice allows them.

If there is such a conflict, society cannot maximize individual freedom and at the same time achieve social justice. Society has to choose between the two goals of liberty and justice. Some theorists and concerned citizens emphasize one; other theorists and concerned citizens emphasize the other. The two groups fight each other, and we get neither maximum freedom nor justice.

◆　　　◆　　　◆

But even if this conflict didn't exist, there is another reason that would appear to force us to talk about justice. Since we can see that freedom admits of degrees, it now makes sense to ask how the level of freedom of one person compares with the level of freedom of another person. Should people have an equal degree of freedom? Should a person's degree of freedom be proportional to the person's merit?

In the past, this question did not arise or was trivial if it did. If "freedom" meant non-interference and could only be present or not (and individuals were either completely free or not free at all), then everybody in our society is free and that's the end of it. The freedom of one person equals the freedom of another person.

But we've shown that this simplistic notion of freedom is not adequate, so it is possible to ask how the level of freedom of one person compares with the level of freedom of another person. In other words, we must confront the concept of justice.

Definitions of justice

The number and variety of theories of justice over the ages is impressive, and it would require several volumes to survey them all. The meaning of "justice" is as hotly contested as the meaning of "freedom." Some people hold that justice means treating everybody equally, paying everyone an equivalent wage, for instance.

But other people disagree, and they have some cogent reasons to offer. The value of the jobs that people have to do to get their wage is not the same for everybody. Some jobs are easy, enjoyable, performed in clean surroundings, and so on, while other jobs are dangerous, dirty, or require the person to carry the fate of everyone in the organization on their shoulders. Some jobs require little preparation, other jobs require long and arduous (and unpaid) preparation before a person acquires the qualifications to do the job. Because of facts like these, some people hold that justice means making the wage fit the job, paying higher wages to some people than to others.

Still other people hold that we need not worry about social justice at all since the market mechanism solves all these problems. If we only let the chips fall where they may, it will be a just distribution. If people are not satisfied, they need only change jobs, work harder, go back to school, start their own business, or whatever. (You can see why a "negative" definition of freedom is necessary to uphold such a view.)

◆   ◆   ◆

Note: the invisible hand

The market mechanism is sacred to those who have been treated well by it, so that it is difficult to get them to see that there is *no support* for the claim that whatever happens in a market economy is just or at least is as it should be. They will point to microeconomic theory (but not to econometrics) and become very indignant. They will acknowledge that the conditions (perfect information, perfect competition, and so on) necessary for the market mechanism to have these desirable characteristics are not met nor even approximately met in the real world; but having made the acknowledgement, they think they can thereafter ignore such trifles.

But in addition to pointing out the ingenuousness of these claims, we can also ask questions about where those chips are falling and why the best of all possible worlds does not appear to be resulting from the market mechanism.

This is not to say that a market mechanism may not, after all, turn out to be the least objectionable way to distribute money, or even jobs. I am only pleading here for an open mind, or at least for an amused tolerance from these true believers.

◆   ◆   ◆

Most of the attention paid to the idea of justice in recent years has focused on trying to decide between these competing definitions of justice. Most theorists did not doubt that political thought needed a concept of justice in one form or another. To claim that one could specify what society ought to be without the use of some concept of justice was inconceivable if not downright immoral. These traditional views are still defended, for example, by Kelbley. Justice provides a criterion for what society ought to be; an ideal society will be a society that is just.

More recently, a few daring philosophers have been more cautious: justice is not an ideal but it is necessary in specifying what society ought to be. Or at least it is helpful in doing so.

Let's look at both these views. If neither of them is justified, we don't need to enter the hornet's nest of controversy over what justice is and how it relates to freedom.

Justice as an Ideal

First, the view that justice provides a criterion for what an ideal society would be.

Does it?

What is meant by an "ideal society?" Everyone will have some favorite ingredients to propose for inclusion in such a society. How can we possibly decide between them? How can we possibly include them all?

Rather than rush in to tackle this question, let's see if we can rephrase the term "ideal society" in such a way as to preserve its meaning but without saying what the actual ingredients of such a society would be. An ideal society would be one which (in plain terms) could not be improved upon, in other words, a society in which no logically possible re-arrangement of the existing conditions and no other additional conditions would constitute a better society.

With this definition, we may not have to spell out what such a society would be: If we can agree on what concrete characteristics would *not* be ideal, then we can recognize what is not an ideal society. Alternatively, if we can show that any proposed society could be improved upon, then we have shown that it is *not* ideal.

The strategy we are going to follow is to show that even if a society met the criterion of justice we would be able to point out flaws in the society, the society could (at least logically) be improved upon. If we succeed in doing this, we have shown that these definitions of justice are not sufficient criteria for an ideal society.

◆   ◆   ◆

Note: distributive justice and retributive justice

The word "justice" has been used to talk about two kinds of things. The current practice is to regard them as two different kinds of justice, but it is arguable whether they have anything much in common other than the fact that the same word has been applied to both. "Distributive justice" is concerned with the question how ought the valued things in a society to be distributed between people. The valued things are money, jobs, space, air quality, roads, etc. "Retributive justice" is concerned with behavior: if Jones's behavior hurts Smith, should some equal or corresponding hurt or punishment be applied to Jones? Or should some other treatment be applied to Jones?

◆   ◆   ◆

To decide whether we need either the concept of distributive justice or the concept of retributive justice in order to specify what an ideal society would be, let's consider distributive justice and retributive justice separately.

Distributive Justice

Distributive justice directs that every person should get his or her due. What is due a person could be specified in the quantities one person receives relative to what another person receives or relative to a job the person does or relative to some other criteria of deserving.

Each of these possibilities sounds reasonable. But what if society does not have sufficient resources to give each person the *quantities* specified? In this case, what is due each person would have to be specified in terms of *proportions* relative to what other people receive or relative to the selected criteria of deserving.

But regardless of whether quantities or proportions are used, the same objection applies: as long as the package a person receives does not include all that she or he wants, then that package is to some extent disagreeable to her or objectionable to her, whatever else it includes. In other words it has to some extent what we might call "negative value."

But in an ideal society no degree of "negative value" would exist. One could always (theoretically) improve the society by eliminating the negative value. As long as negative value exists, society has not arrived at the ultimate goal.

◆　　　◆　　　◆

Note: But what about Pareto?
Of course, if the world is in fact so diabolically constructed that it is impossible to increase one person's share without making another person's share smaller, that is indeed a bad situation; but to label that state-of-affairs as "justice" does not make this bad situation good.

◆　　　◆　　　◆

Hence, whichever criteria of distributive justice are used, they are not sufficient criteria of an ideal society, or even sufficient to govern that aspect of an ideal society concerned with the distribution of the resources of the society.

In a few minutes we'll consider whether any of the criteria of distributive justice are necessary (perhaps along with other criteria) for stating what an ideal society would be. And we shall argue that justice is not a necessary criterion either.

Retributive or Legal Justice

The problems of legal justice concern punishment (or more generally, the proper treatment of criminals), the proper awarding of damages, the proper treatment of broken contracts, etc. In all of these problems the underlying task for legal justice involves the resolution of a conflict between one person and another or between one person and the collectivity of persons (conceptualized either as "the public interest" or as "the state").

But a conflict, however natural it may appear to us now, is not an ideal state of affairs and not part of a goal toward which society should be striving. An ideal society would be—not one in which conflicts occurred and were resolved "justly"—but one in which conflicts did not occur at all. The ultimate goal of society should be the prevention and elimination of conflicts, not their resolution (although provision has to be made for conflict resolution as long as the ideal has not been reached). In conflict resolution, someone always loses, either the plaintiff or the defendant or both. In an ideal society, there are no losers.

Justice in Non-ideal Societies

It might be comforting to notice that we are not alone in doubting whether the concept of justice is necessary for specifying what an ideal society would be. Two eminent thinkers who have rejected this view are David Hume, the eighteenth century philosopher, and John Rawls, the twentieth century political philosopher. Their argument is that if certain limitations, such as scarcity and conflict, did not exist in the real world, justice would be superfluous.

Their position is, thus, more cautious (and harder to refute): justice is necessary for stating what a good, *but non-ideal*, society would be, or at least that it is helpful in specifying such a society. Galston and Hubin are also recent thinkers who have held this position.

If this position is justified, we must still tackle the problem of saying what justice is or of deciding between the many definitions of justice that have been proposed. And having done so, we must then deal with the problem of the conflict between freedom and such a concept of justice.

Since this second position does not claim that societies that meet the criterion of justice are ideal, it is problematic how to assess such claims:

any undesirable consequences could be explained away by being held to be unavoidable or held to be of an acceptable level even though they are unfortunate. I shall argue against this position by (a) questioning the assumptions on which the claims for the necessity of justice rest and (b) questioning the usefulness of the concept of justice as compared to another one.

Assumptions of this position

This position seems to assume that conditions like scarcity and conflict are inevitable. Because of such conditions as these, justice is necessary.

But we should be careful before regarding an existing condition as inevitable and beyond the reach of public policy. It is difficult or impossible to know what is technologically reachable, since the question has to be asked in terms of present-day and near-future technology.

More seriously, the question of what is practicable is often asked with certain other conditions assumed to be unchangeable, for example, conditions such as population size, composition of skills, attitudes of consumerism, and so on, conditions that could in fact change.

Scarcity is inevitable

Consider scarcity, one of the factual conditions that allegedly makes the concept of justice necessary or helpful. Is scarcity inevitable? It has always existed, and there appears on the surface no way to do anything about it.

But there is a difference between a condition's being *inevitable* and its being *difficult to change*.

If people can be persuaded that an attitude of infinite wants (i.e. insatiability) is *necessarily* a *losing* position, since they as individuals will always remain unsatisfied, then they might reassess their attitudes and adopt a structure of wants (a utility function) that is bounded and realistic (in other words, one that *can* be satisfied). In practice, most people probably tend to do that anyway. It is in their interests to do so.

In this case, plenty or satisfaction becomes at least theoretically possible.

Further, if population size is allowed to decrease via the adoption of a one-child norm until the desired size is reached, then plenty becomes a practical as well as a theoretical possibility.

But wouldn't a smaller population mean less production? No. Production, that is, actual or real production, is provided by only a fraction of the population, a fraction that is decreasing as automation increases. Production, then, could be maintained at the same level even as the size of population decreased by minimizing unproductive "service" jobs such as many advertising, marketing and sales functions, and by replacing more clerical functions by machines.

It should also be emphasized that society is only partly responsible for scarcity. Individuals are also partly responsible, since people have some influence on what their wants or satisfactions are. Of course, societal factors like product advertising and life-style advertising influence individuals' wants and these cannot completely be controlled by persons acting individually; society would have to take a hand in controlling such factors.

The point is: scarcity is not inevitable. It might be difficult to eliminate, but people could eliminate it if they wanted to.

Conflict is inevitable

The other assumption on which the argument for the necessity of a concept of justice rests is that conflict is inevitable.

This argument certainly appears to be incontrovertible. Who's ever heard of a society without conflict? As long as you have people, you will have conflict.

Perhaps. But again, the sticking point is "inevitability." Is conflict inevitable? To claim that it is would be to make a very strong claim.

But it is equally hard to prove that conflict could possibly be eliminated. Most people would agree that conflict can be reduced. If so, the question becomes whether conflict can be completely eliminated.

Many conflicts are tied to scarcity. If scarcity is eliminated (meaning that people come to have everything they want) conflict over property should be eliminated. Conflict of other kinds could be expected to decrease as people understand their own wants better, are better able to communicate them, and come to realize that others are more likely to satisfy their wants if they satisfy the wants of the others and are involved with them in relations of equal respect.

Whether conflict is completely eliminable is, thus, at least an open question.

A better ideal or ultimate goal

We have not refuted this second position, that is, we have not shown that the concept of justice is not helpful in specifying what a good but non-ideal society would be.

But we can show that justice is not a necessary condition for such a society by showing that we can specify what a good society would be without using the concept of justice. If we can do this, then we'll have shown that we do not have to use the concept of justice, and therefore do not have to either define justice or resolve conflicts between freedom and justice.

In other words, if we can do this, then even if scarcity and conflict were inevitable, justice is not the only concept for specifying what society ought to be. More strongly, we shall argue that it is not the best criterion of a good society. Even for non-ideal situations there is another concept, different from justice, that can serve the same purposes as justice and that is preferable to a concept of justice.

Let's turn now to this rather tall order. Again, the argument treats distributive and retributive justice separately.

Distributive Justice

In an *ideal* society, plenty prevails. Plenty does not mean that every conceivable product or service exists, but it does mean that every person has everything that she or he wants, present and future. Think about such a situation for a moment. If you have everything you want, you do not want anything else, whether another person has it or not. In such a situation, you do not care whether someone else has more objects than you (as long as you know that the conditions of plenty will be satisfied in the future as well). In other words, the distribution, the relative proportions between you and other people, are a matter of indifference to you as it is to the other members of the society.

Nor does it matter whether what you get is in proportion to how much you produced, since in an ideal society the means by which things get produced would have been re-designed such that jobs no longer constituted a punishment and hence did not need to be compensated by an equivalent proportion of income. People would work as an artist (or a philosopher) works, because the work itself is rewarding. Receiving part of the product of society would constitute an additional good, not a reward for "merit," a compensation for pain and suffering, or an incentive to do an onerous task.

The ideal, then, the ultimate goal of society, is plenty (satisfaction) for all people as soon as possible for as long as possible.

◆   ◆   ◆

Let's look at what such an ultimate goal does for us. In order to reach this goal, the benefits of society must be distributed and they must be distributed to everyone. So, this ultimate goal is not obviously unfair or grossly unjust in the sense of leaving someone out or short-changing someone. Yet, we have not specified anything about the comparative proportions.

But if society does not have sufficient resources to reach the ultimate goal immediately, then what do we do? We have to have intermediate goals. Maybe distributive justice should be an intermediate goal?

Intermediate goals

But the purpose of an intermediate goal is to be a step on the way to the ultimate goal, not a substitute for the ultimate goal. And it is not obvious that specifying constraints on the distribution of resources would move society closer to the ultimate goal. What might some of the intermediate goals be? And would they be as desirable as or more desirable than justice?

Some of the intermediate goals are those discussed above: smaller population, no product advertising, advertising to promote leisure time satisfaction without the self-defeating need for large consumer purchasing, redesigned jobs and working conditions, etc. Intermediate goals are, of course, not ideal; but they should point the way toward situations that are better. These intermediate goals do so, since they are at the same time *means* to the ultimate goal.

The question most pertinent here, of course, is income: The part of society's wealth that is not used for investment must be distributed somehow or other. Should there be among the intermediate goals a criterion requiring some kind of proportionality such as the ones specified by the various theories of justice?

If incomes were more than a little unequal, competition for income would result; and attention and effort would focus on increasing the income rather than on setting and maintaining reasonable satisfaction levels. This would be counter-productive. Equal incomes alone, however, would establish competition for *jobs* unless the jobs could be made to be of equal interest. And if the jobs were of equal interest, competition might focus on the education or training that is required to qualify for the various jobs, the easiest educational route being preferred.

In practice, however, there are ways to avoid these destructive forms of competition. One could allow amount of time spent on the job to vary to account for these differences in desirability: the more disagreeable the job, the shorter the working hours. (This would be preferable to using differences in income, because differences in income tend to become differences in power, and differences in power become even greater differences in income.) Alternatively, each person could have two jobs and spend a certain proportion of time on a disagreeable job and the rest on an interesting one.

Moreover, the seriousness of this practical problem should decrease over time: as consumerism decreases, the amount of time spent at a job of any sort would decrease. And the number of disagreeable jobs should decrease as jobs are redesigned.

All things considered, then, approximately equal incomes *and* approximately equal jobs, together with the other intermediate goals specified here, would probably move people toward the ultimate goal in an acceptably expeditious manner.

With these intermediate goals, society does not need a concept of distributive justice.

Counter-arguments

There are two kinds of counter-arguments to this claim: one is that the above intermediate goals are arbitrary and without justification, the other is that they are merely another theory of justice in disguise.

Most of the intermediate goals described above are clearly not arbitrary. The question pertains to the intermediate goal of equal incomes. I would argue that only an intermediate goal of both equal jobs and equal incomes addresses the ultimate goal of satisfaction *for all* as soon as possible. An intermediate goal of inequality addresses an ultimate goal of satisfaction for *some* as soon as possible.

Another reply to the first counterargument is that an element of arbitrariness could be admitted to, if need be, because one is not trying to say that the intermediate goals are good *per se* or "just." They are steps toward what is good, namely plenty or satisfaction for all.

The second counterargument is in some ways the opposite of this one. It charges that not only are the intermediate goals good, these intermediate goals are really *another theory of justice*. So, I have ended up utilizing a version of the very concept I am supposed to be arguing against. The grounds for this charge are that something is being distributed, that everyone is included, and that equal incomes and job-qualities are distributed to everyone.

On the surface, this appears to be a knock-down argument. Let's take the parts of the argument one by one.

First, all philosophical theories apply to everyone, so this part of the argument is not sufficient. Second, not every theory of distribution is a theory of *just* distribution. An essential ingredient for a theory to be a theory of justice is for it to make a comparison between what one person receives and what another receives (either directly or in proportion to the jobs they do) and that it make a claim that there is something good or proper about those relative proportions. And we not said that there is anything valuable about the comparative proportions between people either directly or indirectly, either at the ultimate goal or at the intermediate goal.

Finally and more importantly, even though we have been talking about distributing resources, we have been doing so because this is a *part* of the ultimate goal. The ultimate goal applies to conditions and activities like the quality of life on the job, the degree of control a person has over these conditions, etc. Some of these conditions can be improved for one person without detracting from another person and hence do not need to be "distributed" in the usual sense. Others can be improved by changes in organization and are thus less dependent on the level of society's resources. Thus, this intermediate goal has broader scope than theories of distributive justice typically have. Also, there are still other intermediate goals, such as the control of advertising and the reduction of the birthrate, that are more important in reaching the ultimate goal than distributing resources is.

But the major difference between this theory and theories of justice is in how the intermediate goal is justified. We are not claiming that the intermediate levels are "just" or even good (although through time people should be better off than they were at previous times, otherwise more effective intermediate goals should be chosen). We are claiming that the intermediate goals are steps in the direction of the ultimate goal. The justification of these intermediate goals is that they are bringing us closer to the ultimate goal.

A normative argument based on justice would have to argue that these intermediate distributions, if they conform to the comparative proportions specified by the theory of justice in question, have something good about them. With the above approach, we do not have to justify comparative proportional distributions *per se*.

◆   ◆   ◆

Note: interpersonal comparison of utilities
Moreover, we are relieved of a problem faced by all theories of justice: making interpersonal comparisons of utilities, a problem whose solution is generally held to be impossible.

◆   ◆   ◆

So, the above counterarguments fail to refute this alternative theory of an ideal or ultimate goal for society. But let's not give up so easily. Isn't it an argument against the above intermediate goal that there might be some other way of generating the intermediate goal that would make more people better off? For example, "the greatest good for the greatest number." In other words, make as large a majority as possible as well off as possible.

No. Such an argument presupposes some other ultimate goal than the one above, a goal such as: to make a majority better off. Other such ultimate goals are conceivable, but such goals would in my opinion be impossible to justify. The goal is to get everyone there, not to get a majority there.

So, given an ultimate goal like the one we have been considering, distributive justice is not necessary for specifying what a good society would be. Would it be *helpful?*

My answer is negative: Distributive justice sets up spurious objectives such as the relative *proportions* distributed rather than the *amounts* distributed. You cannot spend proportions; you can only spend amounts. More seriously, distributive justice is indifferent to the important question of *how expeditiously* a society is approaching the goal of plenty.

Finally, there are two practical considerations: Concepts of justice tend to focus attention on the compensation people receive for the (perhaps inhumane) work they do rather than on re-designing the jobs themselves to improve their quality and the freedom of the person doing the job.

Secondly, enforcing particular proportional distributions may be difficult since some people might on their own initiative increase their own proportion, rendering the relative proportions "unjust." One could argue that they are free to do so and freedom is good. But such an argument would miss the point: the claim of justice is that *the distribution itself* (the relative proportions) has some value. Therefore, their changing this distribution would be immoral or undesirable.

Legal or Retributive Justice

If retributive justice holds that the person who causes pain to others must suffer an equal degree of pain himself, this could be a means to some other intermediate goal, such as minimization of conflict (in this case, by deterring others from committing crimes), and hence a sub-goal; but is it *necessary* to have retributive justice as a sub-goal?

No. There are other means of reducing conflict: for example, the reduction of scarcity would be expected to reduce conflict over property. Also, conflict prevention (as discussed in the chapter on Limiting Freedom) is an important means of conflict minimization. Other means include psychotherapy for criminals, and the like.

Is retributive justice *preferable* to other non-ideal goals or sub-goals? This question recalls the debate between the advocates of punishment and the proponents of other treatment procedures for criminals, such as psychotherapy, family therapy to attempt to prevent the development of criminals, elimination of poverty and other social conditions thought to promote conflict, etc.

Without getting into this debate, we can point out that it is one thing to say that punishment is a means of minimizing conflicts and another thing to say that retributive justice is. To call the practice "punishment" is to say that it is regrettable but helpful; to call it "justice" is to say that there is something good about it in itself. To regard the introduction of pain as good seems a mistaken way of conceptualizing the matter (and similarly with other kinds of treatment). Political philosophy would be clearer and less paradoxical without such a concept.

◆   ◆   ◆

There are other conflicts, conflicts in which liability is not an issue, conflicts which are not caused by one of the persons involved. An example would be conflict over a sharable resource such as a giant telescope. For such cases of conflict, the concept of distributive justice might appear to be a more useful one than retributive justice. For example, taking turns could be viewed as equal distribution of a prima-facie non-distributable resource over which there is a conflict.

But the question is whether there is something good or right which is being achieved in such conflict resolutions. Someone is still being temporarily denied a resource. Isn't the justification rather that since neither party is able to support an exclusive claim to the resource, there is no other rational way to resolve the conflict than to distribute the resource equally?

And when there *are* such claims that a society might choose to recognize as a basis for granting priority (for example, that only astronomers be allowed to use certain scarce radio-telescopes), it is not clear that the criteria on which such claims are based need to be criteria of justice. Does the astronomer "merit" the telescope or is it merely rational that only qualified people use it?

Conclusion

In conclusion, justice, however defined, is not an ultimate goal of society. The goal of society is to move beyond justice. This is not to say that the ideal society would be unjust. It is to say that the goal is to produce a society that will make justice irrelevant. I have not shown that justice *cannot* be taken as a non-ultimate or intermediate goal; but I have shown that it is unnecessary and unwise to do so.

Consequences

There are two important consequences of the elimination of the concept of justice from political theorizing. One of these is of interest only to philosophers and is presented in a footnote.

The other consequence is that society no longer has conflicting goals, justice on the one hand or freedom on the other. This conflict is a serious problem, both practically and theoretically. If liberty and justice are in conflict, we cannot have both as ultimate goals, we have to choose between them. But this choice would be an arbitrary value judgment. Hence, we cannot choose. (Hence, in practical terms, we are without a goal and cannot justifiably act.)

With the elimination of justice as an ultimate goal of society, the conflict vanishes. The alternative conditions which I have suggested *are* the ultimate goal (such as plenty for every person, present and future, absence of conflict, and control over these conditions by the individuals themselves) are precisely the conditions defined in this book as freedom.

Why we should accept this view of freedom

The views that have been put forward so far in this book may seem plausible, but their seeming plausible is not a sufficient justification for accepting them. Various persuasive techniques of language can make the reader (can indeed make the *author*) believe a statement even though the statement is not true, and the same holds for moral or normative claims. We need some reason, some grounds for accepting these claims. How can we provide such support?

What is a justification?

What does it mean to give a reason for accepting a set of claims and when are these reasons sufficient? Everyone has an intuitive understanding of what it means to give a reason for something. Now, we must try to make that intuitive understanding explicit and clear.

Ideally, what we mean by sufficient reasons is a proof of the sort found in Plane Geometry. In such a case, the statement we are trying to prove follows necessarily from the other statements we use to support it. This works because these other statements have already been proved by still other statements and those statements are tautological.

Outside of mathematics, however, these methods by themselves are not sufficient. We cannot find useful tautologies to start with, and to start with statements that are not tautologies begs the question we are trying to prove.

How then do we proceed?

One class of statements other than tautologies that have been successfully used in other fields are statements of the form: If such-and-such conditions occur, then so-and-so will happen.

The way of justifying statements like this is by setting up such conditions and then seeing whether the predicted result happens. If the predicted result always happens, we can have some confidence in our statement. But we cannot be absolutely certain. After all, the next time we try it, it may not work.

In practice, however, subjecting these statements to such tests have enabled us to build precision machines, go to the moon, cure diseases and accomplish much else. When suitable precautions and controls are used, the possibility that it might not work next time has not had serious practical consequences. We can even operate with statements in which the predicted result only happens ninety-nine percent of the time.

It is important to emphasize, however, that we have not *proved* these statements in the sense in which theorems in Plane Geometry are proved. And there are people who do not accept such statements even when they are sick and their lives depend on their accepting them. (Of course, they often pay for their lack of acceptance with their lives, but that is their affair.)

The point is that such statements are justified in some sense other than that in which theorems in Plane Geometry are justified.

The reason for emphasizing this point is that the kinds of statements we are dealing with in this book, normative statements, are different from *either* of the two types of statements just discussed. It would be surprising if either of the above types of justification could be used for these statements. Normative statements guide actions rather than describe situations.

But if these two long established kinds of justification are inapplicable to normative statements, what kind of justification *can* be used? This is the problem that has stalemated ethics up to the present time. My answer is this: Just as the human race worked out a new kind of justification in the process of working with statements of the form: If **x** happens, then **y** will happen, so we will have to work out a new kind of justification in dealing with statements of the form: **T** should be the ultimate goal of society.

(And just as there are people who will not accept a given statement of the former kind even when the amount of evidence is overwhelming, so there will be people who will never accept statements of the latter kind no matter what the consequences may be. The theory of justification they are accepting (often without knowing it) is the Plane Geometry type (the deductive model) and nothing else will do. What they do not realize is that, even if a deductive proof *could* be given for a normative statement, it would do no good because the statements used in the proof (the premisses) would have begged the question at issue.)

In sum, deduction is a proof; but it is not support, not a justification. The premises presuppose the conclusion, the statement to be supported, and thus beg the question.

Inductive evidence is support, but it is not a proof.

The justification that I will be offering, then, will be neither a deductive proof nor a preponderance of empirical evidence. The justification I offer, then, will have to be evaluated for itself, not rejected mechanically simply because it is neither a deductive proof nor an infinitely repeated scientific experiment.

What, then, is support in connection with normative or action-guiding claims? Support for an action-guiding claim is a set of statements that give us grounds for acting on the claim. Such support enables us choose those imperatives that help us carry out our purposes successfully and helps prevent nasty surprises. Support in ethics should perform the same function: provide us with grounds for action. The support I offer for my definition of liberty fulfills this function.

Is it impossible to justify normative claims?

To motivate this discussion of a new kind of justification, consider the following: It has been argued that it is impossible to justify normative statements. It isn't simply that no one has been able to do it, it *cannot* be done. The reason is that normative statements are not what they appear to be. They appear to be ordinary descriptive statements: "You ought to do **x**." In fact, they are not declarative statements at all, they are prescriptive statements. The person who says them is really saying: "Do **x**!" No set of declarative statements could ever justify that sentence, because it is a different kind of sentence.

Other philosophers have disagreed with this claim. But without going into the long history of this debate, it is possible to show that this debate is beside the point. To illustrate this, consider a statement that is admittedly not the same kind of statement as the one we need to justify here: "You ought to buy shares of XYZ stock."

Now, whether I am goading you or guiding you, may be a question of interest to philosophers. It is not a question of interest to you. The question that is of interest to you is: Should you buy XYZ stock?

Further, suppose the following declarative statements are true: (1) Today, the price of XYZ stock is five cents a share. (2) Tomorrow, the price of XYZ stock is one hundred dollars a share. (The fact that we learn that statement "(2)" is true when it is too late is beside the point here.) The point is that *if* I know that statements (1) and (2) are true, I know the answer to my question: Should I buy XYZ stock?

Moreover, these statements have all the force of one of the kinds of proof above: they support or provide grounds for my action of buying XYZ stock. Anyone who knows these statements and is still asking whether to buy XYZ stock is either insane or has not understood the argument. And this is exactly what we say of someone who does not accept a deductive proof.

Prudential versus moral

Philosophers will argue that the statement, "Liberty as defined here ought to be the ultimate goal of society", is not the same kind of statement as, "You ought to buy XYZ stock." The latter is called "prudential", the first "moral." They can, of course, not prove that the distinction they are making is justified, because that proof, like all others in this realm of discourse, is subject to the same problem we are discussing here.

Yet, philosophers fervently believe it and reject anyone who proceeds under the assumption that the distinction does not hold.

For the sake of argument, I shall accept the distinction between prudential and moral statements.

Justifying freedom versus justifying the accuracy of the definition

In stating my theory of liberty, I have used a lot of words, made a lot of claims. What exactly is it that will be justified here?

At first glance it would seem that we have two problems: one is justifying freedom itself (Is freedom really worth anything?) and the other is justifying this particular definition of freedom.

But until you say what you mean by "freedom", you cannot justify "freedom" (as you define it). It is freedom or liberty *as defined* that must be shown to be valuable, that must be shown to be so desirable that we as a society ought to adopt it as our ultimate goal. For example, if "freedom" merely means "negative freedom", then the process of justifying it would be very different from the one here (and I don't think it can be justified—in other words, I think any attempt to justify it would fail). To put it another way, if you don't have a justifiable theory of liberty, your attempts to justify it *should* fail.

Justifying the theory of liberty T

The crucial points in this theory of liberty that have to be justified are the following: (1) that each person should decide and control his/her own actual (as opposed to perceived) interests, (2) that every person counts, and (3) that each person's own or "self-regarding" interests are (part of) the ultimate goal of society. A separate claim, one that we shall also argue in favor of, is that this theory of liberty should be given the label "liberty", in other words that the ordinary English word "liberty" is an appropriate label for this theory.

We shall take up these points in the reverse order from the way they were listed above. Once again, what we are trying to support or justify is the claim: The state-of-affairs specified by theory **T** should be adopted as the ultimate goal of society.

Self-regarding interests

The claim is: A person's self-regarding interests are (part of) the ultimate goal of society.

What is meant by a "self-regarding interest"? Briefly, this term refers to anything which benefits a given person, call him **I**, regardless of whether or not it benefits anyone else. Further clarification of this term will be presented below.

I will make three separate attempts to support this claim. Each one of these attempts might be (and I believe is) sufficient to justify the claim. Refuting (or rejecting) one of these claims, then, is not enough. To refute the justification of this claim, all three must be shown to be insufficient.

Self-regarding reasons versus moral reasons

The claim here is that the ultimate goal of society should be the benefit of each person in the society. Why is that problematic?

For most people and indeed for most political scientists when they engage in political theorizing of a normative sort, and for some practicing politicians trying to support their favorite governmental programs, such a claim is *not* problematic, and to question it causes raised eyebrows. But some philosophers, religionists and perhaps others have traditionally argued that there is a difference between self-regarding interests and moral interests, and hence that to offer self-regarding interests (or benefits) as a reason for doing something is not to offer a moral reason and hence fails to be a justification for doing a particular action or adopting a particular policy. Indeed, this difference is regarded in philosophical circles as so well established that to deny this claim would itself cause raised eyebrows.

However, while I would agree that a distinction can be made in language between self-regarding interests and moral interests, I will now argue that the attempt to separate the two fails.

One argument that could be used in the attempt to separate the two holds that self-regarding reasons refer only to present or near-future consequences while moral reasons take into account long-term consequences as well. But it would certainly be in everyone's self-interest to make decisions taking into account all consequences (although the trade-off between long-range and short-range consequences still has to be made). So, this attempt to separate self-regarding interests from moral ones fails.

Another attempt could claim that a moral interest is one that a person would follow if the person had all the relevant information, whereas a person acting to further his/her own self-interest is acting under limited information. But it would certainly be in a person's self-interest to have all the relevant information and to use it in making decisions. So, this attempt likewise fails.

More seriously, one could distinguish between self-regarding actions and other-regarding actions and claim that moral reasons are ones that take into account both types of actions and that sometimes oblige a person to engage in other-regarding actions rather than self-regarding ones.

Let's look more closely at this notion of an other-regarding action. Is there any such thing as a *pure* other-regarding action? It is not obvious that there is. For instance, when Jones does something for Smith, Jones usually feels better for having done it.

But there is a more serious problem with this argument. First, let's ask the rather philosophical question: Is an other-regarding action one that furthers the self-interest of the other person? As usual when asking philosophical questions, we consider both possible answers:

If not—that is, if an other-regarding action does not further the self-interest of the other person—should we not be opposed to doing it? Far from being a morally required action, such an action would appear to be morally reprehensible.

If so—that is, if an other-regarding action does further the self-interest of the other person, and if these are the sorts of actions that we are saying are morally required—then everyone is obligated to perform such actions. But if everyone does other-regarding actions, then everyone benefits! In other words, doing such other-regarding actions is in everyone's self-interest. Hence, the difference (though not the distinction) between self-regarding and other-regarding breaks down.

In other words, there are self-regarding reasons for doing other-regarding actions.

Another argument has it that moral reasons are those that have to do with developing "character." This argument hides a lot of considerations inside the word "character." Presumably, the kind of character that moral actions develop is one that engages periodically in other-regarding actions. In this case, this argument becomes equivalent to the previous one. Or "character" might refer to delayed gratification. This would be admirable provided the overall or lifelong benefit to the person is maximized. But if it is, then this advantage is already contained within the definition of freedom being supported here.

In the past, there were arguments that moral actions were those that accomplished **x**, **y**, and **z**; but **x**, **y**, and **z** did not give the actor or the recipient of the action anything that they particularly wanted or that benefited them in any way that could be made clear. Fortunately, such arguments are becoming more rare these days.

In sum, the distinction between self-regarding interests and moral interests is dubious at best.

The costs of being wrong

But suppose now that we accept, for the sake of argument, the difference that we have just been arguing against. In other words, let's grant that there is a difference (and not just a distinction) between self-regarding reasons and other-regarding reasons. And let's grant further that self-regarding reasons are not equivalent to moral reasons. And let's grant finally that the claim "This theory of liberty ought to be adopted by society" is a moral judgment and not just a prudential normative judgment.

I will now argue that, regardless of whether these three assumptions are granted or not, one can still justify the claim that a person's self-regarding interests ought to be taken to be (part of) the ultimate goal of society.

The argument turns on what it costs us if we are wrong. In applied science, the costs of being wrong vary with the application. For instance, if a building is built based on incorrect statements and the building falls, the cost of these statements being wrong is the cost of the building.

With regard to a set of moral prescriptions, the costs of being wrong can be quite high. Witness Ivan Illych's agonizing moment of insight as he is dying: "What if my whole life has been a mistake?"

With the present theory of liberty, the costs of being wrong are zero. This is so because the theory is set up in such a way that nothing is lost if the theory is wrong. In fact everyone is still better off. (This is because the theory is based on maximizing the self-interests of every individual person in the society.) Hence, even if the theory were "wrong," it would still be prudent for everyone in the society to adopt the theory and to put it into practice.

But doesn't this argument beg the question? No. We are freely admitting here that "costs" are prudential or self-regarding. The good reasons, the rational reasons for deciding to adopt this theory are the same as the rational reasons for making any other decision: they are prudential or self-regarding. The claim in question: "A person's self-interest *ought to* be (part of) the ultimate goal of society" can be regarded as either a moral normative claim or a prudential normative claim.

It does not matter, since we are not saying that this claim follows deductively from the statement: "Adopting the policy that each person's self-interest be (part of) the ultimate goal of society costs each person nothing even if the statement is wrong." (Similarly, the statement "We should build the building in accordance with statements s_1, s_2, ..., s_n" does not follow deductively from the statement: "If the building falls, it will cost us a million dollars").

Similarly, to ask for a justification of the justification is to misunderstand the nature of the argument. Again, I am not claiming that the theory follows deductively from the reasons in favor of adopting it as a practical policy. Moreover, the justification (the costs of being wrong) is not surreptitiously posing as a moral theory. It is freely admitted to be prudential, self-regarding, and "rational" in the usual decision-theoretic sense.

To sum up, then: To the question, "Can there be good rational reasons for accepting this normative theory?" the answer is "Yes, by looking at the costs to I of being wrong in accepting T compared to the costs to I of being wrong in *not* accepting T." Again, this does not beg the question since no deductive relation is being asserted between the statement of costs and the theory T.

Testing the justification

Skepticism is the position that one does not know whether any normative claim is justified, hence no one knows what to do. Since even a position such as "Have no social policies" or "Have no government" is a normative position as much as "Adopt social policy x", it is logically impossible to avoid acting in accordance with a normative position. And acting in accordance with a normative position can be taken to be equivalent to accepting it. Hence, one could claim that in the area of social policy, skepticism is incoherent.

However, suppose no ethical or moral position had yet been justified. Who should decide what to do? To give any person's name in answer to that question contradicts the assumption of skepticism.

Since some action must be taken, even if the action is to do nothing, someone must decide. If in default, one says "Let each person decide", this answer is (more or less) equivalent to liberty.

Moreover, ethical skepticism would suppose both of the following statements to be true: (1) There are no good reasons for accepting the statement that "the good of **I** *is* equivalent to the self-interest of **I**" and (2) There are no good reasons for accepting the statement that "the good of **I** *is not* equivalent to the self-interest of **I**". If both these statements were true, people would then have to decide on some basis other than "good reasons". Why not, then, opt for a basis of decision that brings them some benefit?

Non-exclusion of persons

The theory of liberty given here is meant to apply to every person in a society (indeed, to every person on the planet). In more technical terms, you could substitute any given person's name for the variable **I** in the above formulations and these formulations would still be justified.

Is this claim justifiable? Can we justify claiming that each and every person should be included?

In the United States we have been taught for so long that discriminating against individuals is wrong and that every person counts, that to make the claim that every person should be included would appear superfluous and to deny it nonsensical.

But again, some claims have been accepted for hundreds of years which later turned out to be false (for example, that the earth is flat), or turned out to admit of alternatives (for example, that parallel lines never meet); and sometimes claims that appear obvious turn out to be very difficult to support, a clue that should make us suspicious.

So it is with this claim. What reasons are there to include every person? Why not leave somebody out?

The first issue I would raise in attacking this problem is the issue philosophers call "burden of proof:" which side should have to prove its position? In other words, we can turn the above question around and ask, What reasons can there be for *excluding* a person?

Aside from special cases (like criminals), no one has been able to justify a claim that any given individual or class of individuals should be excluded from counting as one of the I's to whom a theory like this refers. People who have attempted to do so have been fighting a retreating action for the last hundred years: first, those who exclude people on the basis of race had to concede defeat, then those who would exclude females, and today, those who would exclude children are retreating (though they have by no means surrendered, since the admitted limitations on competence of children render them in need of protection and aid).

◆   ◆   ◆

Along with the question of whether any individuals should be excluded is the question *who* the excluded individuals are to be. Any theorist who claims that some individuals should be excluded ought to be able to name those individuals or to give us some criteria for picking them out.

The question that would immediately succeed such a naming would, of course, be the question: why? Why should these individuals be excluded?

Not even the most confirmed "devil's advocate" wants to be put in the position of having to answer these questions. Instead, the devil's advocate simply demands that we support the claim that each and every individual should be *included.*

My answer to this request is as follows: No effort to justify a theory such as a theory of liberty can ever succeed as long as some individual is omitted. There can never be a reason why the person whose interests are being excluded should accept the theory that excludes them.

(Remember that we are talking about interests here, not about who should decide what those interests are or how to go about satisfying them. We discuss those questions next.)

People have historically accepted theories that were contrary to their interests. People are still doing so today. But attempts to formulate a reason why they should accept them have never succeeded, and the whole enterprise should make us as suspicious as the attempt to persuade persons to buy land in some far away, unspecified and undescribed country.

So, even if we could think of some reason to exclude Jones from the benefits of a theory of liberty, we would in the very act of doing so, make it impossible for ourselves to state a reason why Jones should accept the theory. In other words, we would have made our own theory impossible to justify universally or to all persons.

A theory that does not hold true (or justified) for all persons is not a justified theory, it is simply another platform in power politics, and should be treated as such.

Individual control

This part of the theory of liberty holds that each person should (ideally) be able to provide at will his/her own self-regarding benefits. (Remember that we are talking about an ideal, about an ultimate goal or criteria of society. Limitations of physics and limitations of technology as well as the necessity to coordinate between different individuals will limit the extent to which people can control their own outcomes.) To put this part of the theory in the more intuitive form that got the concept of liberty into trouble in the first place: people should be able to do what they want.

In other words, the issue here is not whether self-regarding benefits should be part of the ultimate goal of society, but whether the individuals themselves should be the ones to control how and when those benefits are provided. For instance, what if there were some mechanism that could provide each person with what he/she wanted when he/she wanted it (but a mechanism over which he/she had no control whatever, direct or indirect)? Wouldn't this be just as good a society?

Such an ideal has come to be known as "paternalism."

Paternalism

Paternalism is perhaps the only challenger to democracy that remains under serious consideration today. What is wrong with it?

Let's begin by looking at the argument by which paternalism sought to "get its foot in the door", that is, to make itself plausible: expertise. Some people know more than we do, even about our own benefits. Shouldn't these people decide for us? The paradigm example is the case of physicians. Surely it would be suicidal for a person (who is not a physician) to decide his own medical case, prescribe for himself, etc. The physician, moreover, does not decide for himself/herself, does not prescribe the medication that would be best for his/her own case; the physician prescribes what is good for *us*.

Shouldn't an entire society be operated the same way?

Plato is a prime example of this theory. The philosopher-king is wiser than anyone else in the society, and is wise enough not to be at all interested in or motivated by worldly gain and is therefore incorruptible. What better society could there be?

To begin to assess paternalism, let's look again at our more homely example of the physician. We trust physicians to prescribe for us. Why? Because they know about our bodies and we don't. But that is only part of the reason. They have the relevant information, and *we assume they are honest*! What if physicians were like lawyers?

When we ask what it is that keeps physicians honest, we realize what shaky ground we are on. And of course, not all physicians *are* honest.

Furthermore, physicians are licensed. They can be licensed because we agree what is the relevant medical expertise. Who is to license the philosopher-king? What is the relevant expertise that he/she must have? In other words, how do we recognize that Jones is the philosopher-king? Suppose Smith claimed *he* was.

(It has also been claimed that representative government is an inge-
nious combination of and compromise between democracy and paternalism. But the attempt to show that elections meet the requirements
for selection of experts can hardly be carried out. Legislators are hardly
experts who have met some criteria of licensing. The other way of trying to justify representative government is as an approximation to
democracy forced on us by the demands of timely decision-making and
the necessity of solving the aggregation problem. This makes representative government an attempt at "implementation" (in a sense to be
explained in a later chapter) rather than a theory in its own right.)

In order to be able to select the person or persons who can be the
"pater" of a paternalistic society, we have to know what the qualifications are that such a person must meet, qualifications of knowledge
and intelligence as well as qualifications of honesty and beneficence. It
might be possible to state such a set of qualifications; but there is also
the problem whether any human being could ever meet them. (It is
also debatable whether the members of a society could recognize such
qualifications without having them themselves. Do non-physicians sit
on licensing boards and determine whether a given physician is qualified?)

(You also need to consider whether the person appointed as "pater"
would remain honest and what to do if he/she did not.)

This raises the question whether some future super computer could
not fill the role of the "*pater*" of a beneficent paternalistic society. It is a
contingent matter whether the computer could be made to have the
requisite intelligence. It could certainly have the knowledge base and
access it swiftly and decide quickly. It is also a contingent matter
whether the computer could be made incorruptible (for example,
whether its password could be made un-crackable). The computer
hardware and software would also have to be made bug-free.

Such a society would approach that putative ideal: government by
law, not by men.

Just how many of our decisions would this beneficent computer make? It could call us up at seven o'clock in the morning and say, "Okay, Jones, it's time for you to do your exercises now." Even if it is good for Jones to do his exercises at that time, does he want to be ordered to do them? Does he even want to be reminded to do them?

Perhaps the computer-king could deal only with public goods, collective benefits. If it made these decisions and issued orders to those whose job it was to carry them out and enforce them, the arrangement would certainly save everyone a lot of time and worry.

Relevant here are the arguments in the entire second half of Mill's **On Liberty**.

One could point to the benefits of self-reliance. Even feeling a certain sense of responsibility for macro-social affairs might benefit the individual. It would certainly benefit the society. Because, even with a computer-king, the computer has to be guarded, protected. In order to make the social system resilient, resistant to tampering, the people in the society have to share the responsibility for maintaining it. Otherwise, the computer-king would not stay incorruptible very long.

One is reminded of the situation of the ancient Greeks under the Roman Empire. They lost the habit of self-government; and even though they were given a degree of liberty under Rome, they had lost the will to defend themselves, so that when the Roman Empire crumbled, the Greeks were unable or unwilling to defend their cities against attacks by barbarians from the north or attacks by barbarians within their own society.

Another kind of argument is whether this computer-king hypothesis is really an instance of paternalism. Isn't it really just a way to solve the aggregation problem and the self-regulation problem? In other words, is the computer really a beneficent ruler or just the implementation of the practices that a democracy has decided to put into place to govern itself?

The difference seems academic.

In sum, the attempts to show that skepticism is preferable to accepting the theory of liberty **T** fail. Moreover, accepting the equating of the prudential theory **T** to the moral theory **T** is in everyone's interest; not doing so is to everyone's disadvantage. The theory **T,** then, should be adopted as the ultimate goal of society.

Justifying the claim that theory T is "liberty"

As pointed out in the first chapter, when we are proposing to define a word like "liberty", a word that already exists in the language, the meaning we give to the word should not differ too much from the meaning the word has in ordinary usage. Otherwise, we might have a very useful theory **T,** but why call it "liberty"?

The first point to make is that in a real sense it does not matter what label, if any, is given to the theory **T**. What matters is whether the theory is justified. I have now stated reasons why the theory *is* justified. We could call the ultimate goal of society by any name we like and it would still be in the interests of every one of us to make it the ultimate goal of our society.

But the meaning we have given to the word "liberty" is extremely close to the ordinary, unsophisticated notion of liberty. Freedom means being able to do what you want to do when you want, be what you want, have the living conditions you want. What we have done is to clarify the meaning of the word by making its terms and conditions explicit. Making the conditions of freedom explicit has also enabled us to show that this definition avoids a number of philosophical objections that have been raised against the concept of freedom, objections which led philosophers to propose a variety of restrictive definitions. Some of these restrictive definitions actually influenced the beliefs that citizens had about freedom. But fortunately, people have not changed their minds about freedom to such an extent that the original concept is unrecognizable, although for all we know that could happen over time if present trends continue.

In some discussions of the meaning of the word "freedom", a great deal of emphasis is put on the present aspect of the problem, as though if one could show that the meaning of "freedom" that one is presenting is identical to the meaning the word has in ordinary speech, one would have proved that one's own definition is the correct one, and that therefore one's theory **T** is justified. Much argumentation and discussion are aimed at this point.

First of all, such discussion is misplaced, since there is nothing sacred about the way the word is used by speakers of the English language or by any subset of such speakers. The fact that speakers of English have a certain word does not mean that the state of affairs to which that word refers ought to be adopted as an ultimate goal of society. Second, the meaning which the word freedom has for some speakers of the language differs from the meaning the word has for other speakers, as empirical research has shown. So, the above task is a hopeless one to begin with.

Since we have not had to greatly modify the ordinary meaning of the word "freedom" in order to formulate our theory **T**, there is no question that our definition applies to the word "freedom" and not to something else, so this aspect of the task of justification is not really a problem for this definition.

And as pointed out, it is the theory that counts, not what we call it.

Conclusion

A normative political theory is a recommendation to society. And the justification of a political theory is a set of reasons stating why a society should adopt the theory. We have pointed out that our theory **T** should be adopted by a (every) society, because it is in the best interests of every member of society to adopt this theory. No other theory can make this claim (without being equivalent to the present theory).

Conditions that make us more free

We've discovered two features of a situation that define how free we are: the options we have (and know about) and the value of those options to us. These enable us to say how free we are in a given situation. But how in this (each) situation did we come to be just this free and not more so? What are the conditions that affect these two features that define our level of liberty? It is through changes in the conditions *affecting* our level of freedom that we can become more free.

Since level of freedom depends on the availability of options and their value (as well as our knowledge of their availability and value), anything which has an effect on (a) the availability of the options or on (b) their value or on (c) whether we know about the options and their consequences has an effect on our level of freedom.

Obviously, any kind of physical limitations affect the options available. Cave-ins, falls into crevices, being locked in a room, broken legs, lack of a hammer, lack of gasoline—all of these obviously affect what options are available to me in a given situation. (But again, not every option is one I want to do.)

Another condition which has an immediate effect on my freedom is, obviously, my *health*. Feeling poorly decreases the value of all the options available. Being in poor health makes some options unavailable.

Another immediate condition of freedom is *space*. For most people this takes the form of having a home: a house, an apartment, a room of one's own. Such a space relieves us, whenever we choose, of obligations to other people as well as of their scrutiny, criticism, or whatever. And most of the things people want to do require at least some space, whether it is a seat in a cinema, a field to play ball on, or enough room for a chair to sit in to read.

But these conditions are themselves affected by still other conditions. To illustrate with some obvious examples: The amount of space available to each person is affected by (among other things) how many people there are. A person's health is affected by conditions in the surrounding space, such as garbage collection, pollution, health facilities, the state of health of surrounding people, and so on.

These conditions are in turn affected by still other conditions. To continue the previous illustration: The amenities in one's space are affected by the productive capacity of the industries in the society, one's job and rate of pay, and so on. And these conditions in turn are affected by the state of the economy, the level of personal taxation, and so on.

Philosophers call such linkages "causal chains." One condition is caused by another which in turn is caused by another. Two things should be noted about causal chains: (1) the further back we go, the more general and pervasive the conditions we are talking about, (2) the further back we go, the less sure we are of what the cause is, what the effect is, and how much of an effect there is. Also, typically social conditions have several contributing causes, so the causes actually form a "tree," not a chain. This makes it difficult to keep up with the causal contribution of each condition.

But we can be reasonably clear about the immediate conditions of freedom. Let's begin with some of the immediate conditions and then indicate some of the conditions that affect these immediate conditions. For ease of keeping up with these conditions, I have organized them into categories: interpersonal conditions, psychological conditions, economic conditions, organizational conditions, political conditions, and informational conditions. This separation into categories is artificial, since causes and effects are no respecters of abstract boundaries; but the division does have the advantage that most of the information we have about these causal relations comes from academia which has most of this information divided into similar categories.

Interpersonal conditions

When the possible sources of interference with our activities are human, the level of freedom may very well be less than in cases in which the source is nature. Nature cannot deliberately counter our every action or attempt to control us, as people can. Hence, the ongoing presence of human antagonists may well make a situation less free. This is one reason that surveillance makes us less free; the amount of information which antagonists have or can get and its usefulness for interference are factors which decrease our level of freedom—whether the interference ever actually occurs or not. In these ways privacy increases our level of freedom.

In many discussions of freedom, "other people" are routinely treated as a hindrance or a threat to the freedom of the individual. It is said that a person must give up some of his or her freedom for the sake of the advantages of sociability, love, etc.

Some of these discussions assume that freedom means "negative freedom." If the only conditions relevant to freedom are interferences and lack of interferences, then other people are either irrelevant to my freedom or they are interfering with it. Even if another person provides me with an option I did not have before, that is said to be irrelevant to freedom, since "freedom" only means non-interference.

Other discussions depend on a one-sided analysis of the situation. The usual analysis is: we have an individual, we have other individuals. How do we get them together?

The reality is quite different. To begin with, all of us are born. Our values are interwoven with another human being from the very start. Most of what we want is given by another person. Our freedom is provided or withheld by this other person.

Doesn't this put us in a very vulnerable position? Indeed it does. And some people do not get a very high level of freedom even at this stage. And the consequences of that treatment have a serious impact on the person from then on. Another person determines the level of freedom we have by determining what options we have, what their value or interest level is for us and to what extent we are allowed to pursue them.

But the other side of the coin is that the options that we want are given to us (free of charge) by another person. And many of those options, in the beginning especially, *are* the other person herself, the touch of her body, the milk of her breast. Our freedom, figuratively speaking, is the other person.

Also, our level of freedom is bound up with hers. If she is happy, she is apt to provide an environment in which virtually everything we do makes us happy. If she is irritated, much of our exploratory behavior will be met with consequences which we do not want.

To begin with, then, our level of freedom is bound up with another person and with her level of freedom. Far from constituting a hindrance to our freedom, then, another person provides our freedom. We would have little or no freedom without her.

Similarly, when we are children, we prefer to play with other children. Our most valued options are provided by other children, just as we provide theirs.

There is nothing utopian in these statements. This is simply the way it is. The fact is, then, that other people constitute a possible source of increases to my freedom as well as a possible source of decreases to my freedom. And we must recognize both if we are ultimately to arrive at policy recommendations for increasing freedom.

Let's begin with the positive.

Cooperation

One form of co-operation has been called "back scratching:" If you do this for me, I'll do that for you. This type of co-operation can occur between people who are not even friends or who have no other interest in each other. It can cover bartering, selling personal property, as well as trading favors or services: You baby-sit for us today and we'll baby-sit for you tomorrow.

Another type of co-operation is planning activities together. Consider a simple activity like dancing. Although it is theoretically possible for people to dance by themselves, people tend to prefer to dance with another person. Other examples include trips, picnics, parties, dates, studying together. Many of the things that people want to do can only be done with other people or are more valued when done with other people.

The Dyad

Although co-operation may occur between any number of people, most of the features relevant to freedom in these situations can be found and analyzed in the two-person group known in social psychology as "the dyad."

Let's consider a simple activity that could be done alone, like going to a movie. John can go to a movie alone. Mary can go to the same movie alone. They can also go to this movie together. Going to a movie is an interesting case because watching a movie would appear to be a solitary activity. You do not talk during a movie. And assuming that you do not hold hands or engage in any other contact or communication during the film, you would appear to be doing something by yourself.

Why then does John often prefer to see a movie with Mary?

The value that we experience from an activity, even a "solitary" activity like watching a movie, is often increased by experiencing it with someone else. Why this phenomenon occurs is a fascinating question. But the only thing that need concern us at this time is that it does occur. There are many activities which have increased value when done with another person.

Also, remember that we value not just activities but situations. We enjoy *being with* another person. In other words, the situation of being with a particular other person has value in itself.

Perhaps what is involved here is merely that we are experiencing two values at the same time: being with another person *and* seeing a movie. But I think it is more than that. I believe that being with the other person not only has value in itself but that it *increases* the value of seeing the movie, so that we are not only experiencing two values instead of one but that one of those values is greater than it would have been by itself. Perhaps because we are experiencing the movie as we experience it and also experiencing it as we imagine the other person experiences it.

If the other person also values the experience (likes the movie) and expresses this enjoyment, this too increases our enjoyment of the experience.

Moreover, having many such good experiences together increases the value of the other person. We value the other person more than before for having shared a valued experience together.

In technical terms, there is a positive feedback loop at work for us here: having the experience with a valued person increases the value of the experience, the positive value of the experience increases the value of the other person, which increases the value of the experience, etc.

To avoid other people is, thus, to miss out on all the valued options that other people make available.

The fact that our values are related in this feedback fashion can also work against us: having a bad experience with a valued person can decrease the value of the other person, especially if that person is the cause of the pain.

Of course, another person can cease to have value for us (we can stop liking them). In that case, the enhanced value of experiences shared with this other person does not occur. In this case we usually stop seeing the other person. In other words, the dyad terminates. When the dyad terminates before one of the people has stopped valuing the other person, that person usually experiences greater or less pain.

Beliefs about the other person and perceptions of the other person's motives can influence one's valuation of the other person. Consequently, anything which affects these beliefs and perceptions can influence our freedom. The classic example is Othello.

Group status

We make a conscious distinction between friendships and groups. Groups, such as relationships, marriages, roommates, families, etc. represent relatively more frequent or relatively longer-lasting interaction patterns. Usually, entry into the group is marked by some major event: having sex in the case of a relationship, moving in together in the case of roommates, signing a legal document in the case of a marriage, the birth of a child in the case of families. In contrast, friendships are characterized by fluidity: people gradually become emotionally closer or drift apart as their feelings and experiences together change.

Why do we make this distinction? Since people feel that they are committing themselves to some extent to more frequent or longer-lasting interaction by entering a group, they are more hesitant and more careful about doing so. As a result, one person may be ready to enter into the group status before the other person is. The other person may never become willing to. And one person may want to leave the group status before the other. Thus, groups can represent a source of pain and disappointment for people.

What is it that group status provides its members that the informal or unspecified status of friendship does not? Does it really prevent people from drifting apart? Does it make them more willing to try to "work out" their differences rather than simply drift apart? Does it reduce the uncertainty about the other person's availability?

People who value their friendships tend to put forth some effort to "keep them up." But people in dyads can do the same. Also, persons in a group tend to cease to consider the option of destroying the group (unless such an option is forced upon them).

In the past, marriage was set up in such a way that the option of leaving the group was unavailable or extremely costly. This is no longer so. But having children creates a financial burden on both the father and the mother which, for people of ordinary financial means, reduces the number of other options available to them. Also, the time required by children when they are young further reduces the options available to the parents. These reductions in options must, of course, be balanced against the additional options provided by the existence of the children themselves when deciding whether children represent a net gain in freedom for the parents or a net reduction.

When people in a group share a space, this may affect the freedom of members of the group. To the extent to which the environment in that space is what a given person wants, to that extent the person is more free or less so. Some of the members may want the space filled with the sound of rock music, others may not. Some may want it so at times when others do not. This conflict frequently characterizes the group consisting of parents and their adolescent children.

The value of other people

We have hundreds, perhaps thousands, of criteria for judging other people. Other people must measure up on features major and minor. Height, weight, hair color, interests, all are specified. Some of these criteria we are aware of, others we are not. A woman may despise male chauvinism, yet respond strongly to a macho male. (Macho males have figured this out and now talk a good "women's lib" show.)

Yet, when other people judge *us*, we want to be judged "for ourselves." We do not want the color of our hair or our height or our weight to be used against us.

This creates a profound and extensive scarcity in our social worlds. There are few other people we find "attractive." And not many people find us attractive either.

But there are so many human beings in the world, that we tend to treat this problem as a search problem: the task is to find the right person. People have developed more or less elaborate search techniques. We go to parties, we join organizations, we volunteer for committees, we place and answer "personal" ads in magazines and newspapers, we register with matchmaking agencies.

The problem, however, is that no one could possibly measure up to our requirements completely, nor can we to theirs. We need to sort out the few characteristics that are important, and we need to respond to these, not just cognitively but emotionally as well. The extent to which this is possible is not known.

Correspondingly, we need to change ourselves, to make sure that we meet the few important characteristics that a person we want would desire. Again, this may require deep changes. People now are willing to change their clothes or their hair style; they are willing to use make-up and go to aerobics. Beyond this, they do not want to change. They want to be judged "for themselves."

Of course, at bottom it remains to some extent a search problem. Whatever our criteria, we must find other people who meet them. For this purpose, technological aids could certainly be developed or improved. Many people still refuse to use personal ads or matchmaking agencies. This reduces the effectiveness of these search techniques enormously. In addition, there is a semantic problem implicit in these intermediaries: how to specify in words what relevant characteristics a person has, and what characteristics the person is really looking for. Some people are mistaken about what their own characteristics are. Many people's perceptions of their own characteristics are influenced by what they would like to be. People are sometimes mistaken about what characteristics of others they actually respond to. And finally, there is the problem that anyone who actually measured up to the characteristics sought would not want the person doing the seeking: in other words, people want someone so good that such a person would not want them.

Typically, people measure up on some characteristics and fail on others. People begin a relationship because of the former and end it because of the latter. Through heart-to-heart talks and through psychotherapy people can try to change their requirements that other people must measure up to, and can try to change their own characteristics (and not just their clothes) so that they meet the more important of the other person's criteria. Most importantly, people must learn to realize what they really want in another person and to change that requirement if it is unrealistic or self-destructive.

Bribes and threats

Of course, other people can also decrease our level of freedom. They can interfere with what we want to do. They can compete with us and win the prize we want to win. They can eliminate some option we would like to select.

Two of the most interesting ways other people can decrease our freedom, however, are threats and bribes.

A *threat* is someone else saying, "If you do **A**, I'm going to make sure the consequences are bad."

A threat can involve occupational conditions such as being fired and blacklisted (that is, prevented from getting other jobs), being fired without being blacklisted, being transferred to a less desirable position, and so on. If someone said, "Hand over your money or you're fired," we would probably feel more free than if he said, "Your money or your life."

What all of these threats have in common is that they involve the manipulation of the value of the alternatives.

Nothing we have said so far rules out these situations. We still have options, the options have valued consequences. Yet, something is wrong here. This can't be freedom.

What is wrong is that the other person in this case is, in effect, choosing for me. You could say that he is forcing my choice, although this would be a paradoxical way of putting it, since the word "force" and the word "choice" mean the opposite of each other. In other words, this is not a choice. There is an element of force applied to the choice situation itself.

The question is: are we free to a certain degree in these situations or are we not free at all?

Under situations of mild threat, we may still retain some degree of freedom; but our freedom is decreased by the presence of the threat. Under situations of severe threat, we are not free at all.

◆   ◆   ◆

A *bribe* is someone saying, "If you do **B**, I'm going to make sure the consequences are good."

A similar point is discussed variously by de Crespigny, by Price and by White.

Usually, the word "bribe," however, is reserved for situations in which the action **B** is not what I want to do or is even reprehensible. If someone says, "If you sell me your house, I'll pay you a million dollars," we would not call this a bribe. I can either sell and buy another house, find another buyer who will offer me more, or stay where I am. But if someone says, "If you sell me your wife, I'll pay you a million dollars," we would usually consider this a bribe.

On the other hand, if situations of this kind are ruled out, then freedom would be incompatible with cooperation!

Bribes that put us into approach-approach conflicts, that is, situations in which we want both of two options, one of which is being rendered unavailable by the bribe, do decrease our level of freedom. Also, remember that people can experience negative value and positive value simultaneously. These experiences are two separate dimensions, not just one, and thus do not cancel each other out. Men want a gift of a million dollars, but they do not want to sell their wives. However, unlike threats, we can always say "no" to a bribe; so, we still retain some level of freedom.

Threats and bribes can be offered at the same time. The cases of the infamous "offer you can't refuse" are of this type.

Several factors determine how much of a decrease in freedom is caused by a bribe. One is the *costs* associated with the option to which the bribe is applied. These costs include the amount of time the option takes, the amount of effort, any unpleasant side-effects, etc. A person who does a job he hates for pay has his freedom decreased a great deal. A person who does a job he likes for pay does not have his freedom decreased at all.

A second factor is the value of the second-best option. (We have already said that a bribe has to make an option the most preferred one, otherwise we simply laugh and ignore the bribe.) If the option is one we would never choose without the bribe and the alternative is starvation and death, our level of freedom is very low. A person who has to have a job in order to eat and can only get a job he hates is in this situation.

A third factor is the possibility (or probability, zero or more) that the option may cease to exist in the present or in the future. How much this decreases our freedom obviously depends on the value of the second-best option. To take a different example from that above, if we have a choice of bribes and if the other bribes are nearly as good as this bribe, our freedom would not be much lower, even if the present option is undependable.

How likely it is that an option may cease to exist depends on a number of factors: whether the person offering the bribe may himself come to be unable to offer it in the future, the availability of other people who could provide the same service we are being bribed to provide, and the extent to which the person offering the bribe needs our services. (We know he needs them to some extent, otherwise he would not be offering the bribe.) For example, in the early days of computers, programmers were in great demand. No threat whatever was associated with job-loss. And correspondingly, programmers were treated very, very nicely by their bosses.

Finally, if the threats or bribes are of unknown value I may be less free than if the value is known. Similarly, if these threats are attached, not to specific commands but to unspecified and ubiquitous prescriptions and proscriptions, a person is in a situation of an extremely low level of freedom. For example, a junior manager who works for an irrational and unpredictable boss is sometimes in this situation, as are children with inconsistent parents.

◆   ◆   ◆

Another consideration peculiar to helpful behavior, however, is the non-zero probability that it may be manipulative, that it is really intended to influence us or that it may lead to consequences that are not in our interests. These possibilities decrease the level of freedom that we have while faced with an offer of help. When does an offer of help increase our freedom and when does it decrease it? It would seem that if the offer stems from shared interests, our level of freedom is greatest (other things being equal), for example, if friends extend an invitation whose acceptance would please them as well as us, or if two persons are exchanging something valuable to them both. When the offer is charitable, it may not last or may not recur, and when the offer is self-interested only, it may have unknown disadvantages or side-effects present or future or may decrease our future freedom (for example, it may make us dependent on someone who may become an antagonist). These factors must be considered along with the others in determining how free we are in situations in which options or information are provided by others.

◆   ◆   ◆

But threats and bribes are not the only way a situation can be set up by another person. Suppose someone gives me two tickets to the opera for Saturday, and going to the opera is more attractive than anything else available to me on Saturday. And suppose the other person gave me tickets to the opera in order to get me out of the house, so he could rob my house. The issue, then, is not whether the situation has been contrived, but whether it has been set up in order to get me into another situation where I can be clobbered.

◆   ◆   ◆

Some social situations are deliberately set up in such a way that one of the objectives is to lower the freedom of the other person. For example, the game of chess. Perhaps a similar statement could be made about economic competition.

Persuasion

Persuasion has a problematic, and therefore philosophically interesting, relation to freedom. If Mary persuades John that disposable diapers are better than the old-fashioned kind, has Mary limited John's freedom?

If we say yes, we are ruling out education, a form of cooperative and helpful behavior.

In general, we can say no. If John is in fact persuaded, then John now believes that disposable diapers are better and is acting in accordance with his own belief when he chooses to buy disposable diapers.

Persuasion can decrease one's freedom in at least two ways: A person may be persuaded to believe something which is not true. When he chooses in accordance with his new belief, he gets clobbered by the consequences of his choice.

Second, a person can be made to think she believes something which in fact she does not believe. This statement will seem unintelligible to an economist, false to a political scientist, and a commonplace truism to a psychologist. The sad fact is that a person can be mistaken about what she believes or about what she prefers.

It is tempting to claim that if the means used in the persuasion are irrational ones, then the persuasion is an interference with freedom.

But a case cannot be made for such a claim. Irrational arguments work only on an irrational person. And it is true that a person whose thinking is irrational will have plenty of surprises in store when he witnesses the consequences of his choices; hence, a person who thinks irrationally will, other things equal, be less free than someone who thinks rationally.

But paradoxically, if the irrational arguments cause people to hold beliefs which increase their freedom, the irrational means used to achieve that result will not add to their lack of freedom. For example, people in one corner of India were persuaded by the Indian government to exterminate the rats infesting their villages, thus improving their health. Irrational means had to be used because the local people believed the rats to be sacred.

How other people increase freedom

In general, then, other people increase your freedom to the extent that they create options you want, and they decrease your freedom to the extent to which (or the frequency with which) they eliminate options you most want. Some people eliminate more options than they create. Other people are or become neutral to your freedom. You tend to drift away from such people.

In friendships, we seek out people who represent a net increase in our freedom. To the extent that these individuals are available to us we are more free.

What can you do to increase your freedom? How can you have an effect on these conditions such that your freedom is increased?

Improved search capabilities have already been mentioned. Beyond this, one could recommend bringing child-rearing practices into line with what people want. Raising children in such a way that no one will want to be involved with them is not a favor to the children. Similarly, encouraging children to judge other children with a myriad of criteria creates the problem described above. And obviously, if parents judge their own children by a multitude of criteria, the children will adopt these criteria.

Clearly, we do not want our children to adopt a policy of accepting all comers, since they would soon be deeply hurt by the first exploitative person who came along, but just as obviously, the importance of factors like hair-color or eye color are of doubtful value in increasing their freedom.

The role of the mass media in developing such trivial criteria is obvious. But movies, rock groups, and television also promote an attraction for more important characteristics; and some of these may be highly destructive. For example, the practice of rock stars of cultivating an image of a thug—whatever its value in increasing the sales of their recordings—is damaging to many of their adolescent "fans." These young people, in seeking a relationship with someone who has the mannerisms, appearance, and language of a thug, may actually get a thug.

Causation and the acquisition of values

Where do our values come from? What causes us to value one thing and not another? What causes us to value one thing more than another?

It should be remembered that not all wants are caused by someone else, physiological motives being the most obvious exception. Also, circumstances sometimes condition a person in such a way that the person acquires a (positive or negative) value. The point is that a value is no less a value for having been caused by another person.

Causing the acquisition of wants clearly does not reduce freedom in the following cases: first, causing someone to value freedom itself cannot decrease the person's freedom (unless the definition of "freedom" that the person is caused to value is restricted).

Second, causing the valuing of conditions which increase the level of freedom (or of actions leading to such conditions) cannot decrease freedom. As seen later in this chapter, this would include causing the valuing of increased self-regulation and increased information, the valuing of increased flexibility (hence, more interests, fewer needs, etc.).

Third, causing another person to value something does not affect that person's freedom if the priority that person places on the object is so low that the person will never choose that object.

On the other hand, there are clear cases in which causing the acquisition of values does decrease freedom, for instance, causing the acquisition of values which conflict with existing values (unless these are at the same time eliminated).

Second, causing the acquisition of values which can only be satisfied at great cost or ones whose consequences are costly. The point here is that to the extent that the options we value are costly or difficult to satisfy we will be less free.

We are also less free if an enjoyable action has painful consequences: the proverbial hang-over, for example.

These points have implications for education as well as for child-rearing. Since education and child-rearing create some values and shape others, persons involved in these activities must consider the future freedom of the people (the children) they are influencing and use the criteria above in deciding which values to encourage and which to discourage. To try not to encourage or to discourage any values will not maximize the children's freedom.

Psychological conditions

So far, we have treated human beings as rather simple entities with wants, with information concerning the extent to which various options are available that satisfy those wants, and with the ability to more or less rationally weigh the different alternatives.

This oversimplification must now be corrected. People are more complex than that. The value of the options available to us and even the options themselves are influenced by factors which occur inside us.

Knowing what goes on inside a person is, naturally, difficult to achieve; but ignoring these internal factors or pretending they are not there does not increase our freedom. Skepticism is useful, but not when it becomes a dogma. Skepticism means doubt. It does not mean certainty that unobservable factors do not exist.

The other extreme—the practice of asserting anything we want about what goes on inside people—is not helpful either. *Believing* that people operate in this or that way will not make it so. And making decisions on the basis of such unreliable information sets us up for some nasty surprises.

What then are we to do?

Fortunately, methods have been developed over the years for gaining information about what goes on inside human beings. It is a slow, painstaking process; and even though it has been going on for a hundred years, it still has a long way to go. Basically, it involves testing one's theories about how people's thoughts and emotions function by observing whether the behavior predicted by one's theories matches what people actually do in various situations. Whatever the limitations of this type of procedure, no one has yet thought of another way, let alone a better way.

What factors, inside the person, are so far well enough known that we should take account of them in assessing how free we are and how we can become more free? The results so far have usually been obtained in association with various theories of personality; and since no one theory has yet emerged that has enough evidential support to become a paradigm, we must present the results available so far in terms of these different theories of personality.

Self-regulation and its limits

There are many experiences which people do not want to feel and would avoid if they were able to. Any experience of pain will do as an example. But people also feel fear, anxiety, guilt, shame, depression, etc. Every personality theory admits the existence of some such experiences, though there is disagreement over what causes these experiences and how they are to be handled.

One's first reaction would be to say that people would be more free if such unwanted experiences were eliminated. But the situation is not as simple as that. If people never felt guilt (as in the case of psychopaths), we would have a society in which the mechanisms of social control would have to be so thorough that very little freedom would be left. And if people never felt fear, they would be unable to respond to cues that call for normal self-preservation.

These experiences, then, are useful in self-regulation and enable a person to avoid other unwanted experiences. Hence, we cannot simply state that a person is more free if unwanted feelings never occur.

What is important as far as freedom is concerned is that these experiences not occur in the absence of the situations to which they are appropriate and useful, and that they not occur to such an extent that they actually interfere with the person's response to those situations.

Unfortunately, both these problems do sometimes occur. In these cases, it is important for the person be able to control or regulate their occurrence or duration. Personality theories disagree over the extent to which people can do so. Merely repressing these feelings, for instance, does not make a person more free, because of the consequences of repression and because the information value of the feelings is lost.

In most personality theories, what may be called the executive (variously called the ego, the self, the will, etc.) is not capable of controlling all that goes on in the person, though it controls the motor activities and to some extent cognitive activities (reasoning, remembering, communicating, perceiving, etc.). Theories that assert the existence of other processes of personality (such as those that produce guilt, etc.) hold these to be largely immune to direct executive influence, although virtually all theorists hold that these processes can be changed with the help of a therapist.

It would not maximize freedom if everything that went on in the personality system had to be done by executive decision, since the system would get hopelessly bogged down. Some degree of non-conscious or automatic functioning is necessary. Still, the idea that the other extreme is true, that the executive is incapable of directly intervening in some processes, presents a model in which the level of freedom obtainable is limited.

Methods of self-regulation

Even if direct executive influence on one's own personality processes is limited, a person can to some extent exercise indirect influence. Some methods of indirect intervention have been studied, including autosuggestion, cognitive re-labeling, self-administered conditioning, verbal self-direction, and stimulus control.

Autosuggestion involves using the techniques of hypnosis on oneself to "suggest" a course of action to carry out. For example, if Mary wants to stop smoking and is having trouble controlling her own behavior in this regard, she can give herself the "suggestion" not to smoke.

Cognitive re-labeling involves changing the verbal descriptions that one has come to apply to a given course of action. In the smoking example, Bill might be able to bring himself to stop applying the macho description to a man who smokes, stop telling himself that it is "cool" to smoke, or that women will find him attractive if he smokes. By trying to rid the action of its supporting labels, Bill makes the activity less attractive.

Self-administered conditioning involves using any of the techniques of classical or operant conditioning to associate the behavior to be eliminated with a painful or aversive experience or to associate the behavior that one wants to adopt with some experience one enjoys, some rewarding experience. For example, Mary might drink something which will soon make her nauseous and then light up a cigarette. Even though she knows it is not the cigarette that is making her nauseous, soon the very thought of a cigarette will make her throw up. As another example, Mary might throw a party to celebrate when she has finished some term paper or other project; or she might praise herself verbally for every journal article she consults in preparing the paper.

Verbal self-direction is the rather time-honored method of simply telling oneself what to do and how to do it. By spelling it out for oneself, the task ceases to be formidable, and by knowing what the first step is, it becomes easier to take the first step. If Bill tells himself to read the instruction manual first before trying the use a device, it may help him to begin using the new equipment.

Stimulus control involves arranging one's own environment so that things which cause one to *begin* a behavior are removed. For example, Mary may remove packs of cigarettes and matches and ashtrays from her apartment and refuse to look at billboards advertising smoking. She may turn her head whenever she sees someone smoking, and refuse to enter smoke-filled rooms. Also, when she feels a need to suck on something, she might use an artificial cigarette substitute to satisfy the need without the harmful effects.

In addition, Ellis holds that some unwanted emotional responses are results of certain beliefs, for example, the belief that if something is wrong one must be terribly concerned about it. Changing these beliefs has an effect on these emotions.

Unconscious processes

The set of factors most often cited as interfering with a person's ability to do what he or she wants is unconscious processes. People outside psychology are so awed by the theory of unconscious processes that they sometimes believe that, due to the influence of unconscious processes, people are not and cannot be free at all. Literary people are especially prone to excel in these lamentations.

But the image these people seem to have of the human personality does not correspond very closely to any theory in psychology, not even Freud's, the one usually cited.

Not every personality theory posits unconscious processes, and in those that do, unconscious functioning is only part of the personality system. Still, it is not unusual for a theory to hold that unconscious processes not only affect a person's feelings but can also: (a) block action (for example, the experience of an artist of being unable to paint), or can (b) impel a person to act, sometimes in a self-destructive way (for example, the compulsive gambler), or can (c) cause one to be unaware of or to misperceive what one's preferences are (for example, the person who thinks he wants to become a doctor). Sometimes, beliefs about what is right and wrong can be so extensive and so inflexible that a person's actions are limited. "The depressed person is imprisoned by unconscious barriers of 'shoulds' and 'shouldn'ts' which isolate him, limit him, and eventually crush his spirit."

Unconscious motives as privileged motives

In the usual presentation of unconscious processes, these motives are portrayed as the villains. They cause people to do what they don't want to do, or make them miserable even when they are doing what they want to do.

Sometimes, however, unconscious motives are portrayed as the ones people ought to be following.

There is no necessary incompatibility in these two views as long as they are referring to different sets of unconscious motives.

The notion that unconscious motives are the ones people ought to be following, though, does present a theoretical problem for freedom. To hold this notion is to claim that some or all of the unconscious motives have a kind of privileged status, that is, that they represent what the person "really" wants to do. If we held this view, we would say that individuals are more free to the extent that they express rather than repress these motives.

To support the privileged-status view, it would have to be shown that unconscious motives always represent a person's highest priorities, or what would be a person's highest priorities under perfect information. At this point, such a claim is not obviously true.

Fromm in his well-known book describes freedom as spontaneity, which he defines as acting in accordance with one's basic motives. What "basic motives" are, Fromm does not make clear. If basic motives are (some or all) unconscious motives, then this is the privileged-status argument above. If not, we have the problem of defining which motives are the basic ones. This is not just a task, but a problem, since such a classification might unwittingly impose our own values and thus pre-empt a person's choice (and do so in the name of freedom itself)!

To my knowledge, no further specification of the notion of basic motives has been made by Fromm. Giving directives to a person to follow this motive rather than that one cannot be done in the name of freedom unless it can be shown that following those directives now will enable the person in the future to be or do what she or he wants more so than not following the directives.

What, then, is to be done about unconscious processes and unconscious motives to make a person more free?

It is clear that one is more free if a motive is conscious than one would be if it were unconscious. And certainly, people can be mistaken about what they want to do. (Hence, we are not dealing here with a subjective concept of freedom nor with perceived freedom.) But once an unconscious motive has been made conscious, should the therapist approve of the patient who chooses to act in accordance with that motive and disapprove (or pity) the one who does not? Or should the therapist try to "free" the patient from the unconscious motives?

Whether Bill acts in accordance with an unconscious motive or a conscious one, the key to whether Bill is doing what he wants to do is the presence of conflict in Bill when he does it. If Bill does what he thinks he wants and then is not happy about it, Bill actually possesses two motives, each of which evaluates the action is opposite ways. Revolving that conflict, and removing the sources of that conflict, will make Bill more free in the future.

Conflict

We have been speaking of wants as though they were unproblematic, but of course they are not. Indeed, the term "wants" is considered too vague to be used at all in psychology and is replaced by various theorists with more carefully defined motivational terms, though these terms differ from one theorist to another.

Most theories allow that a person's motives can conflict with each other. Familiar examples are wanting to do something but not wanting the consequences of doing it (for example, alcoholism) or having to force oneself to do something (for example, to get up in the morning). A person caught in such a bind is less free that if he or she were not in such a situation.

In an approach-avoidance conflict, one experiences something that one wants to experience and something which one does not want to experience. Given a choice a person would prefer the "approach" experience alone to the "approach-avoidance" experience, hence is less free if forced to experience the latter rather than the former. Analogous arguments apply to approach-approach conflicts.

This statement is not inconsistent with the view that people sometimes seek "conflict" or prefer a risky or exciting life to a dull one. A person who most prefers a life of stock car racing, for example, would be most free if able to have such a life. (However, if the risk-taking because excessive or compulsive, the person would be less free.) Similarly, a person who wanted both an exciting life and a quiet one would be less free.

However, personality theories differ over whether and to what extent conflict is avoidable. All theories agree that conflict can be reduced, though they disagree about how much it can be reduced and whether it can be eliminated completely.

But more seriously, some theories, such as Freud's, hold that the experiencing of conflict is necessary for personality development, since conflict is unavoidable and people must learn how to handle it. However, even these theories recognize that a given conflict may be too severe for a given stage of development and that development can be achieved by only a finite (but unknown) amount of conflict, so that more conflict than this would be unnecessary for this purpose.

With respect to these theories, then, we can say that one is less free to the extent that the conflicts are too severe or too frequent, as well as less free in the long run if the conflicts are too infrequent or not severe enough. Too much conflict would overwhelm people causing repression, regression, fixation, or other more debilitating defensive functioning, thus rendering them less able to do what they prefer. Too little conflict would leave people unable to handle conflict and frustration when they occurred, with similar consequences.

It is not to the purpose here to try to decide between these personality theories. Suffice it to say that these theories will disagree over how free a person is and how to promote freedom in this case, that is, the extent to which conflict should be minimized.

Flexibility

One of the concepts used both in ordinary speech and in psychology for distinguishing certain motivating factors is the concept of needs. Different definitions of needs have been proposed by various theorists (for example, Maslow, Murray, etc.) and the alternative meanings of the word have been explored by Braybrooke.

Some of these conceptions make needs and wants almost synonymous. But consider the class of needs characterized by Maslow as "deprivation motivation." Examples given by Maslow are hunger, but also the need for approval. One thing that makes these needs particularly relevant to freedom is the urgency that often characterizes them and their inflexibility (in the sense that substitutions are not possible or are not acceptable).

People with unsatisfied needs are less free than otherwise, since whatever they might prefer to do, they are pressured to act to satisfy the need. It is no doubt this aspect of the matter that has led metaphysicians in the past to believe that freedom must mean escaping from one's wants or mastering one's wants or one's self. (But not all wants are needs of this type; and as we have seen, wants are essential if one is to do what one wants.)

That the flexibility of wants or motives is relevant to degree of freedom can easily be seen. If other people have set up the option that an individual likes most for the purpose of controlling the person's choice, the person in question will be more free if able to decrease the value which that option has for him or her or increase the value of some other option. Similarly, if the most preferred option just happens to be costly or remote, then if people can, without deceiving themselves, raise the value of an available alternative, they will be more often able to do what they want.

Some empirical evidence of change in the value that options have for people comes from research on reactance. Are these only changes in perceived valuations? To the extent that people can by direct or indirect techniques raise or lower the actual value that certain activities or states have for them, they are more free.

A person's priorities are not well-ordered, there are equivalence classes of wants in a person's hierarchy. This permits the person to escape from interference by other people when they control or manipulate one of the valued activities in a particular equivalence class but not others. It also permits a person to overcome the limitations to freedom imposed by the circumstantial arrangement of options in the world; one option may not be available but an equivalent one may be.

To the extent, then, to which a person is willing to accept *substitutes*, particularly in the highest priorities, the probability is greater that the person will be able to do what she or he wants.

Flexibility with respect to the *timing* of gratification of wants also increases freedom, since it enables a person to take advantage of the configuration of options across time. An option may be unavailable today but available tomorrow.

A person's short-term priorities also change due to the fact that as one want or need after another is satisfied, it automatically has a lower priority than another want or need, for example, a person before and after eating. By satisfying a want to some extent, then, individuals might be able to affect their short-term priorities. Grabbing a bite and running, for instance.

The level of freedom, then, is affected by the flexibility with which one can set or change the values of one's alternatives and by the flexibility with which one can select the timing of their satisfaction.

The word "flexibility" could also be used to refer to the ability to change any of the variables discussed in this chapter as conditions of freedom. The extent to which such flexibility of personality functioning is possible is not clear. The concepts of closed-mindedness and of rigidity and authoritarianism suggest limits in the ability to exercise such flexibility for people with these types of personality.

Interpersonal Influence

Many personality attributes such as hostility, perfectionism, paranoia, the exploitative orientation, etc., are likely to find expression in behavior that affects the level of freedom of other people, even if it does not directly lower the person's own freedom. People will be more free to the extent that they do not have to expend time and effort protecting themselves from unwanted actions of others, from pressure or manipulation by others, from irrational games played by others, etc. However, such gains in freedom require not only that individuals select as companions others who are willing and able to renounce such behavior, but that they rid *themselves* of these tendencies, since otherwise their associates will pick up the same behaviors or adopt other counteractions to protect themselves. At best, they will simply ostracize the person.

But there are other attributes which indicate *susceptibility* to influence by others. Authoritarians, for example, are characterized by a submissiveness toward authority figures that is based on need rather than on choice. Such attitudes would be expected to result in lower degrees of freedom on an individual level as well as endangering the societal mechanisms that protect individual freedom at the macro-social level.

Similarly, being external on the I-E dimension should tend to render a person less free than being internal, insofar as externals believe that the world is not amenable to their own control, since such a belief might lead them not to make the effort to do what they want even when they otherwise could. But we cannot say simply that external people are less free than internal ones, since this is only one of the variables relevant to degree of freedom.

People also differ in the extent to which they need other people and to what they need from others. Some need companionship, others need approval, etc. If it is true that the greater the need the more likely it is that people will be doing what someone else wants rather than what they themselves want, sometimes without realizing that their own wants are different, then psychological dependency of this sort is a condition affecting level of freedom.

Perhaps we can distinguish between wanting to be with others and needing to be with others according to the urgency and inflexibility of the motivation. One could conjecture that as the basis of the dependence is increasingly needs rather than wants, the level of freedom decreases (and one would expect reactance to that decrease in freedom to result in increased valuing of independence or decreased valuing of the other person which might actually destroy the relationship). But as the basis is increasingly wants, the level of freedom is less affected or is increased. These are questions which need investigation.

Such dependency needs affect the freedom of the other person also, since the needs constitute demands on the other that pressure her or him to satisfy the need. Again, reactance to this decrease in freedom might occur.

In the theory of Rank, however, increasing the independence of people would increase their fear of separation, while increasing dependence would increase their fear of closeness. This theory, then, implies a limit on the level of freedom which human beings can attain. Whether this result is true of all people is not known. And how many people it is true of is not known. Clearly, reducing the fear of separation and reducing the fear of closeness will be a goal of psychotherapy for persons who have high levels of these fears.

Finally, a common type of interpersonal influence is persuasion. We have mentioned persuasion before, but there are certain kinds of persuasion that rely on the manipulation of personality processes rather than relying on cognitive discussion. Some of the more conspicuous examples are subliminal and other types of advertising, hypnosis, conditioning, etc. It is clear that a person subjected to these techniques is less free at least while under such manipulation than the person would otherwise be. The question is how much effect these techniques have on freedom.

Conclusions

Clearly, the conditions that have been discussed do not exist in a vacuum, other conditions affect them, thereby sometimes decreasing the level of personal freedom and at other times increasing it. The influence of families, peer groups, and society as a whole on the development of needs, on the development of defensive functioning, etc., is widely accepted.

But the fact that factors influence these conditions of freedom does not imply that the conditions are always affected in such a way as to lower the level of freedom. In fact, to increase the level of personal freedom, individuals and society will have to cause these conditions to vary.

What this amounts to saying, of course, is that freedom is not incompatible with determinism. Hence, we may agree with Bay that the metaphysical debate between free will and determinism does not tell us anything about the level of personal freedom. The goal of policy does not have to be to escape from causation but must be to promote causal conditions which increase the level of freedom and prevent conditions which decrease it.

(However, a psychological theory that postulated no executive functioning, no decision-making, *would* be incompatible with freedom—not because it is deterministic—but because, as we saw in chapter two, choice is a necessary condition of freedom.)

In sum, then, the freedom people have is lowered to the extent that their personality processes produce punitive feelings (except for information purposes), contain inconsistent (conflicting) motives, or subvert executive functioning. Freedom is raised to the extent that one's behavior is controllable by the executive, and to the extent that one's values (priorities) can be modified (or held constant) by the executive and delayed or satisfied at times selected by the executive. In other words, to the extent that flexibility applies. Various forms of pressure or manipulation by other persons which operate on depth-psychological variables also, of course, lower a person's level of freedom.

Economic Conditions

Many of the things a person wants to do or to have can be done or had only if purchased. This requires money. To the extent to which one has the money to do those things or have those things or live in those places—to that extent one is free.

This will come as a surprise to no one except philosophers and economic theorists. One would expect conservative economists to be the first to accept this obvious fact, since they are supposedly so much in favor of individuals, of consumer sovereignty, and of all those other good things claimed for market economies. But conservative economists deny this connection between money and freedom. von Hayek calls such a claim a "socialist trick." The reason is that economists accept the "negative" definition of freedom: freedom is non-interference. Whether you have the money to do anything you want to do is irrelevant to them.

Nonetheless, if freedom is being able to do what you want to do, and if what you want to do costs money, you are free to the extent to which you have the money to do it.

Furthermore, most people get what money they have as a result of working at a job. This means that the money you have depends on an organization and on other people in that organization. It also depends to a certain extent on your "performance" (an apt word) in that organization. The extent of that dependence is a matter of considerable disagreement among employees. Most seem to think that their jobs are secure, yet their obedience to the rules and their fear of being *thought* not to have obeyed the rules far outshines the submission of the most fanatical religious zealot.

It is difficult to quantify the degree of a given person's dependence on a given organization. And this is in part responsible for the insecurity that is observable in people's behavior on the job: one never knows how secure one is. Some people feel secure and discover one morning that they no longer have a job. Other people feel insecure all their lives and never get fired. We'll discuss these problems below under the heading of "Organizational conditions affecting freedom."

Another obvious factor determining how much your amount of money affects your level of freedom is the costs (zero or more) of the options you want. If you are like most people, the more expensive the options you want the fewer you can have. An ordinary person who likes horses and sailing is likely to be able less often to do what she wants than a person who likes movies and concerts. (This depends, of course, on the amount of money you have. If you have enough money to do even expensive things, then their price is irrelevant.)

These, then, are the three economic conditions which have an immediate effect on your level of freedom: how much money you have, how much the options you want cost, and how dependable your source of money is. You want to become more free. If you can do something that affects any of these three economic conditions, you will have affected your level of freedom.

First, what can *you* do to increase your level of freedom? Second, what can be done on a group or societal level to increase it?

What can you do? You might try to get more money. If there are more things you want to do than you have money to do, getting more money would obviously increase your level of freedom. On the other hand, if you already have enough money to do what you want to do, then getting more money would not make any difference. (This statement is obvious, but many rich people seem not to have figured it out yet.)

But another way to increase your freedom is to want more things that do not cost money or that cost less. If the things you most want to do don't cost money, then getting more money would not help. To the extent that you can affect your own wants and to the extent that you can acquire a taste for options that are free or inexpensive—to that extent you will be less dependent on money, and less dependent on the organizations that supply money. This statement, too, is obvious, yet most people do not believe it.

People believe that their tastes are immutable, irrevocable, and sovereign over them. Other people believe that to want things that are free is equivalent to self-denial. Self-denial would certainly eliminate the need for money, but it would also mean you were not doing what you wanted to do, and so were not very free. This is not what is meant here. To want something which is free is not the same as to stifle your desire for something that costs money.

Another mistake that people make in trying to increase their economic freedom is to purchase the things that cost less money. The reasoning goes as follows: Here are two versions of the same product. One costs twenty percent less than the other. I'll choose the one that costs less and thus have more money for other options.

This mistake is based on a deception practiced on consumers by manufacturers. The actual situation is this: There are *two* products, not one. Both products are given the same name. Both may even look alike. But one of them is the product; the other is a pseudo-product, a look-alike that is not the same: it breaks down sooner, it does not taste as good, whatever. You are choosing between the product that you want and came there to buy and another product which resembles it and has the same name. Of course, if you want the pseudo-product, you should certainly buy it. But if you want the product, you should buy that.

What has been happening for decades is that pseudo-products have been driving products off the market. Now, if you want the product, you will have difficulty finding it. In many cases, the product is no longer made or grown. In other cases, the product is only available from a specialty shop or through a catalog or on the Web. Some people think this has been happening only to luxury items. This is not true. It has affected everything from shoes to fruits to washing machines.

The only way to stop this trend is for consumers to refuse to buy the pseudo-products. The only way to reverse it is to buy products from specialty shops or order through catalogs or on the Web. (Most catalogs, of course, are in the business of selling pseudo-products.) Reliable and legitimate consumer testing organizations, like Consumers Union, should always be consulted before buying any product they test. There now exist pseudo-testing organizations to help promote the pseudo-products.

◆   ◆   ◆

Besides the things you can do alone to increase your level of freedom, what can be done on a group or societal level to increase it? If economic prosperity and stability increase and if the additional money is distributed to everyone, then you have more money, and (as discussed above) this is likely to increase your level of freedom.

The extent to which this is or is not happening is difficult for the average person to know. The amount of money people are paid usually goes up each year, but what we are concerned with, of course, is buying power, "real" money, as economists call it. Because of inflation, the "real" money you receive each year may not be going up. It may actually be going down.

What you or your group can do to increase economic prosperity is somewhat speculative. Some economists say that increased investment is needed, others that increased consumer spending is, or perhaps both. But the causal chains which connect investment to prosperity are, except in theory, highly probabilistic ones and the probabilities are unknown. In the absence of empirical studies, then, what actions groups or society should take is open to considerable controversy.

Organizational Conditions

The extent to which one or more organizations affects your freedom is the extent to which your membership in the organization is voluntary, that is to say, it depends on the costs to you of leaving the organization. This in turn depends on what values are being provided to you by the organization and the extent to which those values are available elsewhere. For most people, the organization that has the most effect on their freedom is the organization that provides their job. Without the job you have no money. Without money, you have no place to live and no food to eat. In other words, you die.

This extreme threat potential is mitigated to the extent that there are other organizations employing the same skills you possess and *to the extent that those other organizations are in need of those skills.* This second condition is often forgotten both by employees and by theorists.

If other organizations are well supplied with the skills you possess, the fact that you have those skills does not increase your level of freedom. You are entirely at the mercy of your present employer. What each person wants to know is: To what extent is this true of my situation? Usually, you cannot know with any degree of confidence. There are special or extreme cases of course: the early days of the computer industry, for example, in which there was great demand for programmers. But these cases stand out because they are unusual. In most cases, you simply don't know. And the only way to find out is to apply to other organizations for a job. This is risky. Some organizations, though they deny it, fire employees who are known to be seeking other employment.

Of course, government statistics can be consulted; but these are not usually broken down to a fine enough level to be useful to the individual. For, organizations divide skills into very fine distinctions, and having too much of a skill disqualifies you as much as having too little. This fact, too, is not known to the young who have not yet entered the "world of work" or who have only recently done so.

The employment sections of newspapers can also be consulted. Unfortunately, many of these advertisements are intended to give an impression that the company is doing well. Companies that are under a "hiring freeze" have been known to take out full-page ads full of job descriptions. (The excuse is that, when the freeze is lifted, these positions will be available.)

Your range of alternatives, in this case your ease of entering alternative organizations, also depends on how many other people are providing the same skills you are offering. If an alternative company needs two more people with your skills and fifty other people with those skills apply, your dependence on your present employer is great and your level of freedom is very low.

So threatened are most people by this situation (and rightly so), that they are not only unwilling to talk about it, they are unwilling to recognize it. In other words, the psychological conditions of freedom discussed in a previous section play a role in depriving people of this important information.

Finally, your level of freedom depends on the likelihood that you will be forced to leave (fired or laid off). How probable this is depends on many factors, such as how well liked you are, how obedient you are, how well your skills compete with others of comparable skills, etc. No one knows exactly what conditions affect the probability of your being fire, promoted, given a raise or transferred. This degree of uncertainty itself affects your level of freedom on the job, not only because of the fear you feel, but because you are constantly wondering whether there are other actions you should be taking to improve your position.

People (most notably academics) who have never worked in corporations cannot imagine (and do not believe) the range of factors considered by employees and by managers to be relevant to job performance and how minute and ineffable these factors are. Facial expressions, gestures, joking behavior or absence of joking behavior or poor timing of joking behavior, tone of voice—the list is extensive. Social occasions involving diplomats of foreign embassies are probably not more sensitive than behavior within corporations.

Often such things are joked about inside a company, and for this reason people who have never worked inside a company have the impression that it is not a very serious matter. But such joking behavior is a very complex matter and functions to relieve tension, to provide important information for managers, and to give a false sense of security to employees. Even so, the joking behavior itself is ritualized and circumscribed in ways that each employee quickly learns. To transgress against these limits is to risk one's job.

There is also some reason to believe that such minute control is exercised only on white-collar workers and that less skilled employees like secretaries, receptionists, and factory workers can frown whenever they like. But if true, this may only reflect the greater relative availability of secretarial positions at the present time, or may reflect the power of labor unions to be protect factory workers from being fired for "trivial" causes.

Given, then, that most people are more or less stuck in a job and given that most people spend half of their waking lives inside or under the control of the organization, the question arises as to what extent people are free within a given organization?

Obviously, your level of freedom within the organization depends on the extent to which you can do what you want when you want within the organization. Corporations differ widely on this dimension. Different job categories also differ. Some companies have "flexible working hours", that is, employees can come to work at any time they want and leave at any time they want as long as they are in before nine o'clock and don't leave before five. Some employees are given a task to do and allowed to decide how to do it and how long it will take.

Another condition affecting level of freedom within an organization is the extent to which the internal environment and the fellow employees and so forth are what one wants. For example, if the air is full of smoke and you have a prejudice against lung cancer and heart disease you will be unhappy. Correspondingly, if you are a smoker and the company has a non-smoking policy, you will be very uncomfortable (though you may live longer).

Finally, there is the extent to which the organization itself is vulnerable to market and to macro-economic factors such as a sluggish economy or competition from new start-up companies providing the same products or services. Political factors could also play a role, such as tariffs to keep out foreign competition, or easing air pollution standards. Some of these larger conditions are remote and debatable, such as whether raising the interest rate will help the company you work for. Others, even though they are macro-social, have an immediate effect, such as raising or lowering corporate taxes.

Also, we should note that, although organizations almost always cause a decrease in one's freedom, there are people who enjoy what they do within the corporation and could not do it were it not for the company. For such people, obviously, organizations tend to provide an increase in level of freedom. This increase has to be balanced against the conditions discussed above in order to determine the extent to which, on balance, this person is more free or less so. Also, there are rare cases of people who are independently wealthy and work only for additional income or because they enjoy it. For these people, the organization does not represent a decrease in freedom but usually an increase.

Of course, not everyone has an ordinary job in an ordinary corporation. The entrepreneur also has his or her freedom affected by the organization he or she starts. The difficulty or ease of hiring "good" employees, market conditions, etc. affect the extent to which the entrepreneur is free to do what he/she wants. Also, the extent to which the entrepreneur has or can raise additional cash or start a new business if this one fails, affects the entrepreneur's level of freedom.

Mention should also be made of the so-called "free" professions, of which perhaps medicine and the law are the last remnants. Such professionals are similar to entrepreneurs, except that they sell their services rather than produce a product or head an organization to provide a service, and typically they need much less capital in order to enter the market. But they are still subject to the same market forces of supply and demand that an entrepreneur is affected by and are therefore only free to an extent.

◆   ◆   ◆

So, what can you do to increase your freedom vis-a-vis organizations? There is very little you can do. You can try to change jobs, but that as we have seen depends on the availability of alternative jobs. Also, changing jobs too often is frowned upon, and such behavior makes it difficult to get another job even if other jobs requiring your skills are available. Hence, changing jobs is an option that can be used only rarely and at infrequent intervals. And it is difficult to know whether the new job has comparable problems with the old one or has other problems that are even worse.

What, then, can be done? You could try to establish a union. But a union is another organization, in which you would be but a member. Also, the unions that have survived are ones that have restricted their interests to wage rates and length of vacations and in extreme cases to working conditions. Still, unions probably do provide some protection to the individual worker.

Many claims have been made for deleterious macro-economic effects of unions. They are said to sometimes keep wages up and thereby cause a business to fail. The failure of certain newspapers are cited as cases in point. But since there are many causes for the failure of a business, these claims can be and are subject to vehement debate.

Since most people's lives depend on having a job, some people have argued that the only way *life* and liberty can in fact be rights is to establish a legal concept of *job ownership*, whereby a job would be a person's personal property and could not be taken away (except by due process of law). Needless to say, such proposals are bitterly opposed by entrepreneurs and top managers.

If conditions of work on the job are a problem and if too much of one's behavior is being controlled by an irrational or unreasonable boss, one could look to the idea of *organizational democracy* for relief. On this plan, managers are elected by the employees immediately below them. This plan attempts to "have it both ways" in the corporation just as is done in the political system, that is, to have the macrosocial benefits of better control and less costly decision-making by having a few people exercise that control and make those decisions, and at the same time provide those being controlled with some measure of security and of countervailing power.

Obviously, such a plan is opposed by many. Besides the managers themselves who would have to be answerable not only to those above them but to those below them, theoreticians argue that such a system could lead to electing managers for their popularity rather than their competence, and the whole corporation could fail as a result, causing every employee to be out of work. Theoreticians in favor of the plan argue that popularity is already the criteria for promotion and that, moreover, some managers promote those who are less competent so that they will not be threatened by an underling who is more able than they.

Political Conditions

Political systems on the local, state and national level are supposed to provide certain benefits to members of the society. In order to do this, they need funds. The debate centers over what benefits they should provide and how much it should cost. (A "kluge" has been invented as a way of having it both ways: namely, let future generations pay for it, in other words, increase the national debt. One reason our own taxes are so high is that past generations have done this to us.)

Some of the benefits are clear and immediate: political system provide additional options which everyone values or eliminate possible conditions which everyone does not want. Other benefits are weak and the likelihood that they will occur at all is debatable.

Taxation is a condition which, taken alone, immediately lowers every individual's freedom by making unavailable some options which would otherwise be available. Government expenditures, on the other hand, are supposed to increase individual freedom by making available additional options which would otherwise be unavailable. The net result of the two taken together should be a net increase in your freedom, that is to say, you should gain more options than you loose or those options you gain should be of more value to you than the ones you lose.

The goal of a political system should be to make this gain in freedom as great as possible for every individual person.

Traditionally, the benefits provided by the political system were to be ones that benefited everyone. They were called collective benefits. Goods and services that benefited only particular groups (large or small) were to be provided by the economic system. In some cases, benefits which are now provided by the political system do not obviously benefit everyone, or if they do, certainly not to the same extent. Yet, they are still argued to be collective benefits even though the reasons are strained.

There are some collective benefits which clearly and immediately benefit everyone. For example, everyone has a need at one time or another to go somewhere. For this, you need roads. Consequently, building and maintaining roads is a collective benefit. Everyone has a need for water. Providing a water supply and a system for its distribution is a collective benefit.

There are other collective benefits which benefit everyone, but there is disagreement over how much of the benefit everyone needs. For example, most people would agree that some degree of national defense is needed; but how much and what kind of weaponry would be debated. Obviously, the more and the better the defensive system, the more it costs.

Other collective benefits admit of debate as to how much benefit they provide. For example, air pollution at low levels is claimed to be harmless, and therefore preventing or removing these levels of air pollution do not result in increased options for anyone. Others argue that these levels are getting higher, and cleaning the air later will be more expensive or impossible.

There are still other collective goods concerning which there is debate over whether they are a benefit to all people. For example, protecting wildlife.

Debates concerning the above kinds of collective benefits quickly get involved in causal chains. In some cases, these chains can be proved all the way along the line. For example, DDT sprayed on crops causes changes in insects. Eating these insects causes changes in birds (deposits of DDE), causing the birds to become extinct. In other cases, the causal chains have not yet been proved.

There are other benefits which clearly benefit some people, but the extent to which they benefit other people is debatable. As a controversial case in point, consider education. It is argued that taxpayers should pay for education because education benefits everyone. How can this claim be supported?

One could argue that education benefits everyone because everyone has children. Unfortunately, the factual claim embodied in this argument is false, so the argument fails: not everyone has children.

The usual argument is that an enlightened citizenry is necessary for a democracy. Though some unenlightened citizens might disagree with this claim, the claim is true. And discussion usually stops at this point.

But as soon as we examine this situation more closely, we learn something extremely important about collective benefits, something which is true of other collective benefits besides education. To be an enlightened citizen of a democracy, you need to know certain things. You need to understand how your political system works (how it really works), you need to know specifically what it is supposed to be doing for you (and what it is supposed to be doing for the person next to you). And so on.

There are two points to be made here: (1) Not everything taught in public schools contributes to the above information. (2) Not much of the above information (perhaps none of it) is in fact taught in public schools.

The point is this: If the goal of an enlightened citizenry is to be used as a justification for having all taxpayers pay for education, then the education provided should give just the information needed and no more. Students should go elsewhere for other learning, or should pay for it themselves.

If it is argued that all learning which happens to be provided by a given school system is of benefit to everyone in the society, then some other argument in addition to the enlightened citizen argument needs to be made. How does it benefit other citizens? It is in the attempt to answer such a question that resorts to vagueness and extreme generality are made.

It could be argued that those who clearly and immediately benefit from education (besides those who receive the education) are businesses larger than owner-operated ones. Whether this is admitted or not, it is certainly undeniable that these groups benefit more than the public at large. This leads to the obvious prescription that those who benefit more should pay more taxes for education, at least while they are so benefiting. It would in turn imply that families who ask the public school system to educate eight children should pay eight times more than families who ask it to educate only one.

The fact that such obvious results are viewed as not only controversial but vicious and stupid shows the extent to which self-interest influences the cognitive processes of even the most educated people.

This much attention has been given to education because it is typical of other collective benefits. Even collective benefits which benefit everyone do not benefit everyone to the same extent. Claims that it all balances out (you benefit more on this one, I benefit more on that one, and the extent of the two differences in benefit is equivalent) have never been and cannot be supported. A city park near me benefits me more than it does you, and it does not benefit at all those timid souls who are too fastidious to allow themselves to be mugged and will not venture into the park at all. More police protection in my neighborhood benefits me more than it does you. And so on. Sociological research has shown that such inequalities do not balance out. Whether they are proportional to the amount of taxes paid is another question.

The questions that should be asked about every alleged collective benefit, then, are: Is it really a benefit, that is, does it really provide addition options? What is the probability that the benefits, the additional options, will actually result from the government program? How much of a benefit is going to be provided, that is, how much do the people receiving the additional options value these options? And finally, which specific individual persons are going to have their options increased? If these specific questions were asked, legislation would have to be much more specifically spelled out; and many government programs would probably not get funded at all.

◆   ◆   ◆

The other class of results we want from a political system is to prevent and eliminate problems.

Some problems immediately and clearly pose serious dangers for people, for example, crime (the blue-collar variety, not the other kind). Other problems do less damage (at least in the immediate term), for example, pollution. Still other problems have a smaller probability of affecting most people (perhaps, for example, white-collar crime).

It is interesting that the Republican Party has focused on crime as a problem, while Democrats have stressed pollution, etc. The reason Democrats' appeals have been less effective at the polls may be the size of the damage done and the debatable quality of the claims. Welfare payments are, of course, the classic case. Creating ways to show that everyone benefits from these payments has been one of the great indoor sports for Democratic politicians over the last thirty years.

◆   ◆   ◆

Since the justification for any governmental expenditure is the extent to which it increases the options of individual persons, one would think that a great deal of effort would be engaged in by governments to determine what options individuals want. In fact, no such effort is made. Representatives are supposed, somehow, to know. But since representatives make no effort to obtain this information, it is far from clear how they can be expected to know. Still less is any effort made to find out how much people are willing to pay for each alleged benefit.

The situation is certainly strange; some would say, comical. If you walk into a store, you see lots of good things, some of which you might want. But each item has a price tag physically attached to it. You can't miss it. And it is one of the first things you look at. If the price is too high, you don't spend too much time dreaming about that product.

With government benefits, however, the situation is quite different. You walk into one store, and there are no goods there. Instead, a man asks you: "How much do you want to spend?" Naturally, you say, "I have no idea. What am I buying?" You walk into another store. This store is filled with all kinds of good things. But not one of them has a price tag. You choose whatever you want. This situation would not be so bad if, after choosing, you had to go back to the first store and pay the bill. But that is not how the political system works. How much you pay in one store has no discernible connection with how much you buy in the other store.

To make this parable more realistic, we should have the man in the second store *tell you* what you want and how much you can have. You can threaten to fire this man, but only by replacing him with another man standing in front of the store. This other man will then tell you what you want and how much you can have. Even then, you can only fire him if enough people agree with you. And if you fire the second person, your only recourse is to put the first one back in again.

◆　　　◆　　　◆

Mention has been made of the fact that collective goods do not increase everyone's options to the same extent. It should now be observed that some groups or individuals influence the distribution of collective goods to benefit themselves. (If this is not true, then large campaign contributors are making awful fools of themselves.)

It is argued that there is nothing wrong with this. You should simply get together your group and try to influence the representatives too. But one may wonder why it has to be done this way and whether this is the best way to do it. It does appear that a great deal of effort is expended here. If this is not the way you prefer to spend your time, your level of freedom is being reduced just by this requirement alone. In other words, this is another added expense of the system, in addition to taxation.

◆　　　◆　　　◆

What can you do to increase your freedom? In most existing political systems, very little. Write your congressman.

You could get a group together and try to influence the system or change the system. Or you could protest in the streets. But before you do either, you have to know: what can be done to get the system to provide greater increases in your freedom than it now provides?

Some obvious recommendations could be made. One is to provide some way for the government to find out what options people actually want and how much they want them.

Another possibility is to link costs (taxation) with government programs on a one-to-one person-by-person basis. This proposal is subject to what has been called "the free-rider problem."

Another, more modest proposal, is to obtain and publish voter preferences for public services, so that the aggregate preferences of individuals can be compared with what the government is actually providing. The more obvious disparities could be caught in this way, and at the very least, representatives would have some explaining to do.

Informational Conditions

We have seen that knowledge is one of the defining conditions of freedom. If we do not know what we want to do, it is unlikely we will do it. And if we do not know the consequences of our actions, then we do not really know what we are doing: we think we are doing something which has benign consequences, then we get clobbered. This is not what we wanted. Therefore, we have done something we did not want to do.

It follows that one way to increase our level of freedom is to get more or better information about what options are available, about how much we would like them, and about what the consequences would be if we were to choose one or another of them.

But we have also seen that many conditions *affect* how free we are, social conditions, psychological conditions, economic conditions and political conditions. To the extent that we know what these conditions are, as they affect us individually, and to the extent that we know what effects changes in these conditions would have, to that extent we have a chance of increasing our level of freedom (assuming we can alter these conditions).

◆   ◆   ◆

What, then, can we do to our information levels to increase our level of freedom? Clearly, we can try to acquire the above information. In some cases this may be easy. If you know that you like watching movies and you have a good idea what kinds of movies you like, you can order a catalog and a book or two of reviews and rent or buy some movies.

In other cases, the most important information you need may be difficult to get or may be of dubious worth. Knowing what kind of woman or man you are really attracted to or would be happy with, knowing what characteristics you really have to offer such a person—in all of this, you may well be mistaken. Knowing how to change yourself, your tastes, your values, your habits, if you need to—these are matters on which even experts are on shaky ground.

Similarly, knowing what effect various economic policies would have on the economy or what effects various government regulations would have, is a difficult matter. Scientists, even after many research studies, are in disagreement about such questions.

One thing you could do that might help your own individual predicament is to prepare an individual profile of yourself. It would include your own wants, arranged as best you can according to which you most prefer, with some idea how the order of the options changes as one or another is satisfied. It would also include as complete as possible a list of all the conditions (economic, political, social) immediately affecting the options you most want.

This profile would give you a rough picture of how free you are. And in a few cases you might see some easy ways, or at least some feasible ways, to increase your level of freedom right away. It would also show you exactly where you need more information relevant to your level of freedom, and you could set about trying to acquire this information, if it exists.

Comparing your own profile with those of your spouse and children will make it clear why conflicts are occurring between you and perhaps why some of you are quietly miserable even though they are not complaining. Attempting to reconcile these conflicts could avert estrangements later in life. The problems of a society occur in microcosm within a household. It is unreasonable to think we can solve them in a large complex society if we cannot solve them within a seven-room house. Dictatorships, suppression, bullying that passes for paternal wisdom, persuasion and admonition which benefit mainly the person administering it, disenfranchised minorities, secrecy, warfare (using decibels or temper tantrums as ammunition)—all of these features we so deplore in one nation or another can be found in the typical household. And this is to say nothing of the more extreme households, where intrigue, deceit, betrayal and the more dramatic and even violent, forms of conflict can be found.

◆　　◆　　◆

What can be done to increase the information that bears on the conditions of freedom? Evidently, research is what is required. Continuing to amass opinions and unsupported claims, proposed programs with only the author's intuition behind them are not likely to make us any more free in the future than they have made us in the past.

Applying the Theory to the Real World

What we have done so far is to specify characteristics that situations must have in order for a person in that situation to be as free as possible. Each person would like to have his/her life consist of one such situation after another. But the situation I am in next may be affected by something you have done. If I decide to go for a quiet stroll on the beach and find the beach littered with beer cans, paper cartons and remains of hot dogs, or if I find it covered by blotches of oil from the most recent oil spill, the experience is not what I wanted.

On the positive side, many of the desirable characteristics of a situation are provided by other people. If what I want to do is watch television, someone had to produce the programs I want to watch, someone had to build that television set, someone had to sell it to me, and I had to earn the money to buy it. The choreographing of every person's behavior so that it fits together with every other person's is what we call a society.

What we want and what the theory of freedom calls for is a society which, as often as possible, provides situations of maximum freedom for each person in the society. The problem of figuring out what such a society should look like is the problem of implementation. We have a theory of freedom. Now we must implement it.

Theory and implementation

To say the same thing another way: Our theory of freedom specifies design constraints on a society. Now the task is to come up with a design for a society that satisfies those constraints.

And obviously, such a society must work, it must function. It is useless to imagine one isolated situation after another in which an individual is highly free. To take an obvious illustration: John is first in his living room watching television, and in the next instant he is skiing down a mountain. The real world does not work that way. John has to get to the mountain. He will encounter a lot of situations along the way. How free is he is these situations?

Ultimate goals and intermediate goals

A society which satisfies these constraints one hundred percent may never be found. Nevertheless, it is the goal toward which we should be moving. The configuration of individual interests and values may be such that we cannot get very close to that goal, but no one can say for certain that we shall never reach that goal or how close we may ultimately be able to come.

For these reasons, other goals must be found which move us closer to the ultimate goal of a society of maximum freedom. Social arrangements must be found which *approximate* that goal as closely as possible. These goals may be called intermediate goals. In this sense, the question whether we can ever reach the ultimate goal is beside the point. Even if we cannot reach it, the next best thing would be to come as close to the goal as possible.

This implies, among other things, that the ultimate goal would be a society that resolves conflicts of interests in a way that is more advantageous to each person than any other resolution. It is well established that one can imagine or construct configurations of individual interests such that a society that resolved the conflicts between them would not be a particularly enjoyable society for anyone. People must realize this and take seriously the problem. If they cling to every little preference they have, the life that they have will be less desirable to them than if they changed some of their preferences. Individuals whose marriages succeed have probably discovered this already.

The likes and dislikes of real human beings are not as inflexible as one might imagine. Faced with a choice between a society in which neither they nor anyone else gets very much, people would probably prefer to modify some of their own interests to get a society they would like better.

◆   ◆   ◆

One big advantage of applying the distinction between theory and implementation to political philosophy is that we can be more specific about what our disagreements are about. In discussing a proposed social structure or organization, we can be clear that we are disagreeing about implementation, that is, about whether this organization would or would not enable people to be more free (i.e. to do more of what they want to do more of the time). If we conclude that it would not, we do not have to throw out everything including the ultimate goal and the definition of freedom and start over. We simply try to think of another implementation that *would* meet the criteria. Most importantly, when we disagree over an implementation, what we are disagreeing over is a matter of fact. It is not a difference in values. Matters of fact can, potentially at least, be settled by gathering additional information.

It also means that if a mistake is found in a proposed implementation, it does not refute the theory of liberty, it only refutes that particular implementation. When theory and implementation are conflated, if a proposed organizational arrangement is objectionable, the implication is that the theory, the value claims, must be wrong too.

Implementation as a test of the theory

To some extent, the implementation *can* be a test of the adequacy of the theory. If it can be proved that *no* implementation would satisfy the theory, then the theory is useless and has to be changed. Also, if it can be proved that *every* implementation satisfying the theory is a society which has features which no one would want, then the theory has to be modified. If no modification is possible that would result in a justifiable theory, then the theory is useless and must be set aside.

The crucial word is "proved". Simply being unable to think of a satisfactory implementation could be due to lack of ingenuity on the part of the implementor and not due to a flaw in the theory.

The piecemeal approach

To avoid misunderstanding, it is necessary to make clear that intermediate goals are not the same as a "piecemeal approach." In the piecemeal approach, you solve one problem, then you decide which problem to solve next and solve that one, then you decide on the next one, etc.

The problem with the piecemeal approach is that the solution to one problem may create other problems or may change other existing problems. Worse still, the consequences of solving one problem may affect the conditions surrounding a problem you have already solved. For example, your solution to this year's problem may interfere with your solution to the problem you solved last year, so that last year's problem is no longer solved.

The piecemeal approach is the one that tends to be used in a republic, because individual people become aware of one or more problems and become upset about them and pressure their representatives to do something about these problems. Other people become aware of and concerned about other problems. Jones wants no government interference with business because he wants to achieve prosperity for those willing and able to work in an economic organization to get it. Smith wants direct government welfare payments to the poor so that the immediate misery of the poor would be alleviated. (Alleviate the suffering first, then figure out what to do next.)

Unfortunately, the forum for resolving such disputes in our society is now legislative organizations. This is not an appropriate or productive forum for this purpose. First, legislatures have limited or no mechanisms for gathering the kinds of factual information that would enable one to resolve disputes of the second kind above. Second, a legislator's opinions and decisions are often governed by what she perceives to be the immediate or short-term preferences (enlightened or not) of her three constituencies: the voters in her district, her campaign contributors, and the pressure groups hounding her.

Consequently, representatives do not have the information-gathering capabilities to know, much less resolve, the conflicts between these various proposed programs. Moreover, there isn't enough money to do everything the various constituencies want done, so the programs favored by the most influential groups are the ones enacted. As the degree of influence of various groups changes, some programs may be halted and others started. Also, an understandable but totally irrational way of reacting to the insufficiency of money is to fund each program at a level that is too low for the program to be effective. The group which wanted that program is mollified, but the problem does not get solved.

An intermediate goal, then, is not a piecemeal approach, but is a *set* of programs for the entire society which take into account the interactions between the various programs and the effects these will have.

How not to proceed

The usual procedure for a political philosopher or political theorist is to ignore the distinction between theory and implementation and also the distinction between ultimate goal and intermediate goals and to lay out a picture of an ideal society, a utopia. Indeed, philosophers in the past *began* here and did not bother with stating what values their ideal societies were intended to provide.

Philosophers like Plato, Thomas More, etc. started by constructing societies which they claimed were good. But the criteria which made those societies good were usually implicit, or posited, or presupposed. The reaction of many people to these "utopias" has been: "This is all very well, but who would want to live in such a society?"

The approach was wrong because these philosophers were trying to construct the nuts and bolts of a working society without first being clear on the criteria that were to be used to test whether any given feature of that society was acceptable or not. Without such fundamental agreement, discussion of the structures and organizations that should make up a desirable society is futile. We would be disagreeing about what these structures should be, not merely because of the structures themselves, but because we were trying to satisfy different values by proposing those structures in the first place.

It should not be surprising that such an approach has never resulted in widespread agreement on any of the Utopias presented. And for this very reason, we should not be discouraged from trying other approaches (such as the present one) by the fact that the above approach always failed. It was to be expected that any attempt based on that approach would fail.

How to proceed

We are taking a different approach. We have agreed on the criterion that defines a society which can serve as our ultimate goal. We have said that societies are for the human beings living in them and that people want a society in which they have maximum freedom (as here defined), that is, a society in which they have control over getting what they want and have the information necessary to exercise this control without being stuck with consequences they don't want (consequences coming from the natural world around them or from the other people in their social world).

What remains to be done is to lay out the design for a society that could serve as our ultimate goal and to work out successive designs of intermediate goals that approximate that ultimate goal to ever closer degrees.

Good. Unfortunately, no one person can simply lay out such a design. Why?

There is not enough information about how existing societies work, and there is virtually no information about how a proposed society would work. (Curiously, philosophers in the past were not at all deterred by this. They thought they knew how society worked, and they thought they knew how their utopia would work.) Moreover, it would take more than one person to do all the research and make all the discoveries needed to provide the information. Indeed, it would take more than a few people.

What then is to be done? Must we give up in despair?

No. We can get there from here, but we cannot get there in one gigantic leap of faith. There does exist a great deal of information about how various societies function, information gathered by thousands of people working first in the humanities, then in the social sciences and psychology. And of course, more information can be obtained. There are even ways to produce information about how proposed or hypothetical societies would function. I'll show how shortly.

What is required is a research project of the magnitude of NASA.

Proposing a massive research project to find out what is to be done does not presuppose that, once the project is finished, the recommendations would be for massive government spending. Obviously, government spending means taxation (or deficits), and taxation is a cost for every taxpayer and is therefore to be avoided to as great an extent as possible. But there are other costs to all of us, and we want to avoid those too. At the same time, we want to get whatever benefits can be gotten from having a government in the first place, and these benefits must be balanced against their costs, just as the benefits of a toaster in a store must be balanced against its price-tag.

In other words, the costs would be factored in, not left out of the proposed ultimate goal as though they were extraneous factors.

The research programme

What *can* be done at this point is to outline what the research programme would look like.

In the first step in the programme, several research projects would go forward in parallel. Each would focus on a level of analysis, whether the individual level, the organizational level, the neighborhood level, the community level, state, regional, national, or world. We'll need solutions on all these levels.

The second step is model building. For each level, those working on the project must work out what they think might be a model that would provide people with as much freedom as possible (and still function). (Remember that each person's freedom would already take into account the limitations required by other people's freedom.)

A great deal of discussion and argumentation will go on at this stage. Each person working on the project will have to speculate, using all the knowledge he or she has on various aspects of the problem (political, economic, social, psychological), on what the problems will be and exactly what will happen when, and what special cases, especially troublesome cases, will arise or could possibly arise. The model will have to have a way of dealing with all such cases.

Certainly, the people working on the project will be human beings. They will have their preconceptions, their prejudices, their favorite government programs, their favorite issues, their beliefs that certain ways of doing things are right no matter what. But this is not majority rule. They will have to convince the others. And the others are not ignorant, and they are not fools. Campaign-style speeches and slogans will get them nowhere. They are dealing with other experts in the various fields.

Moreover, they can reasonably expect that by the time all the work is finished on the overall research programme, each of them will have died of old age. Any temptation that any of them might have had to feather their own nest will be pointless. In any case, the model will not mention individual people by name, so there would be no way to play favorites. And the goal is to make every person as free as possible.

A model of an individual, for example, would include what the person wants, the relative priority of those wants, the person's options for satisfying those wants, and the conditions affecting those options. What organizational arrangements are best will depend on the configuration of individual wants and abilities. (This is another reason why specifying the societal structures first and then stuffing the individual human beings into them is a poor procedure.)

Once a tentative model has been worked out (or perhaps several alternative tentative models) at each level of analysis, the next step can begin. This step is gathering factual information.

Existing descriptive information will have been pooled so that all researchers will know what the others think the facts are. Each statement will also need to be flagged as to how much confidence the group as a whole has in the statement.

Empirical research, then, can be aimed at trying to increase the level of confidence that can be given to the more important statements or to filling in the gaps in the needed information.

At this point, a curious thing happens. We go back to step two and modify our model. The additional empirical research will have shown us that certain things we thought were true aren't. The gaps that we filled in our knowledge may have totally altered how we see the functioning of an organization or a community. What we have learned may give someone on the team an idea for how the model could be done better. So, we go back to step two, modify the model and argue some more about it.

From here on, steps two and three will go on at the same time. More information will be needed, and as more information comes in, more changes will be needed in the model. As these changes are made, still other information will be needed.

Sound like going around in circles? It isn't. It is a recursive procedure rather than an endless loop. The model is being progressively refined. The kinds of research questions that are being asked are more and more specific and more and more relevant to the purposes of the model (to simulate a functioning society in which every individual person can do as many as possible of the things he or she wants to do).

The word "model" suggests something made of wood. But this model will not be static. It will function, it will do things, and it will surprise its creators. Nor will it be a simplistic mathematical model of the sort once favored by micro- and macro-economists. The model will contain tens of thousands of variables.

Such a model could be represented on paper; but by far the easiest way to represent it is in the form of a software system, a simulation model to run on electronic digital and analog computers.

Once a working model has been produced, the next step is to try it out, observe what happens, watch what happens to various individual people in the model, watch how organizations change, whether they meet their goals, watch how neighborhoods and communities change. Then, the question can be asked: Is this what was wanted? The answer at first will certainly be "no."

What to do? You guessed it. Return to step two and change the model. This will necessitate gathering more descriptive information by means of empirical research. More arguing, more speculation. But eventually a modified model will be achieved. At that point, it will be run again.

The results of this run will send the researchers back to step two again.

Generally, though, the results can be expected to get better with most of the changes in the model. A change in the model in the wrong direction will produce results that are plain for all to see and will require a roll back to the previous version.

It is quite possible, though, that some unexpected result from a running of the model will shock the whole project to its foundations. It may require fundamental changes in the model which render useless many of the refinements that have been put in.

The reason for using a computer simulation model is simply that it is faster and cheaper and no one gets hurt if the model does something unexpected and a few simulated individual humans get clobbered. And the check on the model is all the descriptive information that went into it, information gathered from the real world.

But there is a further check. Once a model, say, of a community has been achieved that seems to present far better results than any community existing in the actual society, an experimental community could be set up with the same design as that embodied in the model. The community would be composed of volunteers, but there should be no difficulty getting people to volunteer. If this community really enables individual people to be much more free than any existing community, there would be a waiting list of people trying to get in. Once the community is set up, the researchers can observe how real people would function in such a community, how much they like it, what they don't like about it, what they wish were different, etc.

Assuming the community is not a total failure, the community could simply remain in existence, if the people chose to remain. After all, they should be better off there than elsewhere. But for the researchers, it's back to step two. They have a list of complaints and suggestions, new insights and ideas. They change the model once again.

Obviously, communities and organizations will be the first models tried out in real life. And probably several models of organizations will have to be developed, varying in size and varying in the type of service the organization provides.

Once highly successful communities and organizations have been set up in the real world, there will probably be no difficulty persuading other communities and organizations to adopt the models: if they hesitate, their members will be clamoring to get out of those communities and organizations and into the ones that have adopted the model.

Issues, problems and constraints

In the process of setting up these models some problems will occur that are already well known, and these will have to be solved.

Also, we already know that whatever the intermediate goals decided on by the researchers and model builders, there are certain requirements which can reasonably be placed on them.

For one thing, no individual may be made worse off in the model that he or she is in the present real world.

Second, if one person was not made better off in the preceding intermediate goal, that person must be made better off in the next intermediate goal. This requires that even those who are relatively free be made more so. In other words, it is not part of the design to hold up some people until others have "caught up."

Third, the relative gain in freedom must be greater for those who are at present less free than others.

◆   ◆   ◆

One general constraint on the various models developed is that they be *self-regulating*. That is, they (a) must be resistant to being sabotaged, (b) must not break down, and (c) must change (to maintain the same or a higher level of freedom for individuals) with relevant changes in conditions. For example, as individual wants change, the society must be able to respond to those changes without breaking down.

Functions

One of the functions that gets performed in a society is allocating certain goods of a society to public use, the remainder being held privately by individuals. The public goods of course have to be paid for, and individuals pay for them in the form of taxation.

Conceivably, a society could have no public goods. Any parks, roads or whatever could be privately owned and admission could be charged to pay for them. The opposite extreme could also be imagined.

It is not the purpose here to try to decide what the division should be between public and private ownership. Nor do I think the researchers should decide this question first and then build a model to embody the decision. The purpose is to maximize individual freedom. In the process of developing a model to do that, some division will be made between public and private. The task is not to develop a "minimal government" nor to do the opposite. The objective is to develop an optimal government, optimal in the sense that the division between public goods and private goods maximizes individual freedom as here defined.

◆   ◆   ◆

The model will also embody a way of allocating goods and their costs between present and future. In a society with a purely market economic system, these decisions are mostly the aggregate of individual decisions on how much they will save (or invest) and how much they will spend. The amount they save is invested by banks in new businesses and expansion of existing businesses for producing future products. In actual societies, a combination of government fiscal policy and market mechanisms determines this. The task of the model is not to represent existing methods but to discover optimal methods.

◆   ◆   ◆

The model will also embody a way of allocating goods and their costs between individuals. This problem has already been discussed in chapter four. Suffice it to say here that whatever model is developed, the result will be that some of the time which the people in the society have will be exchanged for a certain amount of purchasing power for goods and services those individuals want. Ideally, how highly each person's time is valued by the society will influence how much the person is paid for it.

◆   ◆   ◆

The method used by political systems up to the present to solve problems has been to put some person or group of persons in charge of the problem and let them deal with it. For example, we have an Interstate Commerce Commission, we have a Secretary of the Interior.

A variation of the same method is to elect representatives and let them deal with it. This method has the added attraction that the people can be blamed for whatever happens since they voted for the representatives. But voting for a representative is the same as "buying a pig in a poke." No one knows what they will get. The representative himself/herself does not know how to solve the problems, because nobody knows how to solve the problems.

These methods are not solutions to problems, they simply make the problem invisible. There is no justification for such practices, and the most charitable explanation is that it is still done this way from long habit.

Similarly, another method of making problems seem to go away is by voting on them. If you cannot solve a problem, vote on it. Adopt whatever the majority votes for and forget about it.

There is no doubting the value of voting and representative government as a step forward—compared to monarchy and dictatorship. The problem is that voting has come to be regarded as a panacea, a kind of magic, the outcome of which is believed to sanctify whatever decision comes out.

This is a misuse of voting, and does not solve the problem. The point is to discover and carry out the wishes of the people who live in the society. Specious uses of voting do not accomplish that objective. When people do not know the consequences of what they are voting for, the votes they cast cannot be assumed to represent their wishes.

There is little doubt that a society will have to have mechanisms for finding out what people want if the purpose of the society is to enable people to do and to have what they want. But society should use whatever mechanisms are most effective to accomplish this purpose, whether voting, opinion surveys, marketing research, or whatever.

Similarly, there is a problem connected with voting. It has come to be known as *the aggregation problem*. When it is necessary for the people in a given group or in a given geographic location to come up with one and only one public good, the different preferences of the people in the group or location must be combined to yield a single choice.

There are problems with doing that. If the questions are asked pairwise (that is, choose **A** or **B**), and if strengths of preference are not asked, a series of such group decisions might yield inconsistent results.

But there are more serious questions to ask: How often is it necessary to come up with only one public good? And why must a society "start over" every time a decision is made, so that the outcome of the previous decision is forgotten and a completely new aggregate decision is made. In this way, the majority rules indeed. Its wishes are the ones satisfied every time. Why are those whose wishes were satisfied last time not disqualified this time? Why aren't people whose wishes were not satisfied given an equivalent in money or at least excused from the portion of tax that would be used to pay for the public good they didn't want?

It will undoubtedly be the case that the people in the society being constructed by this research programme will have to make group decisions, and these will have to be done by voting. But the fewer such decisions there are, the less often will minorities be created and the less often will some people get nothing, but be asked to pay "their share" anyway.

So, an additional constraint on this society is that the designers should attempt to solve as many problems as possible in the design and not avoid problems by simply saying, "Let the people vote on it".

Problems

There are a number of known problems that have been discussed in the philosophical and political literatures. Some are more relevant than others to the approach taken here.

One is the problem of people who try to take advantage of the fact that other people are playing by whatever rules have been agreed upon.

These people are called Free Riders in the philosophical literature, but I prefer to call them by the name they call themselves, "Smart Guys."

Another problem, not dealt with yet by philosophers, is the type of person who does not go out of his way to harm other people but does not go out of his way to cooperate with others either. He simply lets the chips fall where they may. He thinks of himself as "Cool." He would be as much a danger to himself as to others if he really behaved the way he thinks he does. In fact, he often looks out for himself quite well, while pretending not to.

Finally, there are the non-cooperatives. They are not out to take advantage of anybody, they just can't be bothered to cooperate.

An adequate design for a working society must be prepared to deal with these personality types and others. But these are technical problems, not inadequacies in the theory of freedom.

Conclusion

The purpose of this book has been to achieve agreement about this theory of freedom as the ultimate goal of society, not to evaluate any particular implementation of the theory or to propose intermediate goals.

If such agreement can be reached, a huge step forward will have been made. And the problems that remain will be empirical ones and, however difficult, will be tractable.

APPENDIX

For Professional Philosophers

Additional arguments over the definition of freedom

Two kinds of topics are included in this final section: (1) conditions which may or may not increase or decrease freedom, but at best do so only slightly or which are too dubious to bother the general reader with. Some of these conditions have been proposed as defining freedom by others theorists. (2) Controversies likely to be of interest only to philosophers and political theorists.

It may seem odd to have a section labeled as "controversial conditions." Philosophers will, of course, regard everything I have said so far as controversial. The conditions discussed in this section are ones I do not agree with, and the discussion of the conditions is apt to be too technical to interest anyone but philosophers. But I include them so that philosophers reading this book can find out what my reasons are for not agreeing with these ideas. At the same time, these ideas do not qualify for inclusion in chapter one, since they are not a threat to the concept of freedom itself.

It may be agreed that people would be more free if they could either do or not do something than they would be if they could only do it. However, it is less clear whether people are more free if they have *more than two alternatives* than if they have only two. The concept of option demand in urban economics indicates that people are willing to pay to have options open to them even if they are not sure whether they will ever utilize them, and this suggests the hypothesis that people might feel more free as the sheer number of options increases (at least up to some number).

Sometimes people are given the illusion that they have a high level of freedom by being presented with dozens of "options" most of which have no important differences. For example, having forty-five brands of laundry detergent to choose from instead of six or seven. Such *spurious "options"* merely increase decision-making costs without any important increase in results and are therefore a decrease, rather than an increase, in level of freedom.

Suppose that a number of alternatives a person is interested in are closed or constricted. Other things equal, it would seem that people are more free if there are *no closed out alternatives* than if there are some, even if the number of open alternatives is the same in both cases. This possibility is based on Wicklund's research which suggests that people would react to the closed alternatives in one of several ways, for example, by valuing them more. People who can see either of two films that they want to see but are not allowed to see a third film that they want to see are less free than people who can see either of two films they want to see.

It can also be suggested that the *proportion of open options* to total (acceptable) options is relevant: that the larger this proportion the more free the person is. A person who can attend either of two concerts but not two others that he or she wants to attend is less free than a person who can attend either of two concerts but not a third.

A more general possibility, however, is that a person is more free the greater the *degree of positive utility* of each open alternative and of its consequences and the smaller the positive utility of each closed alternative and its consequences. The things that makes "approach-approach" conflicts paradigms of low freedom is that to approach one alternative is to give up or close out the other. The actual choice is, thus, between the value of **a** minus the opportunity cost of **b**, and alternatively the value of **b** minus the opportunity cost of **a**. To say in the above sense that two options are available is to say that choosing one does not close out the other. Other things equal, this condition of degree of positive utility reaches its maximum when one of the alternatives is the one the person most wants to do or have at the moment, that is, it is his or her goal at that time, or has highest priority for him or her.

It might be argued that in choosing between undesirable alternatives, the greater the degree of negative utility of the least undesirable alternative and of its consequences, the less free the person is. A person with a choice between being exiled or hanged will feel less free than the same person would if the choice were between being transferred or fired. However, I have argued above that persons in such situations are not free to any degree, since nothing they want to do is available.

Another debate concerns whether relative differences in utility of the alternatives are relevant. Oppenheim says "my freedom…is again of no significance to me…[if] I am indifferent between [the two options]." But according to Steiner this is precisely when our "decision freedom" is at a maximum. Oppenheim concludes, "Whether **X** is free to do **x** does not depend on the comparative utility to **X** between doing **x** or some alternative **z**." But Oppenheim has failed to use his own comparative concept. The question is whether one is more free under some configurations of comparative utility than under others. The apparent paradox is this: if one option has greater utility, then the choice is a foregone conclusion; but if the utilities are equal, a coin toss would serve as well. How can we resolve this paradox?

The paradox dissolves when we realize that the issue is not how difficult or easy the *decision* is to make, but whether what we want to do is available in the situation or not.

A set of available options may have hidden consequences for level of freedom if the alternatives or their utilities have been manipulated, that is if someone else has set up these options in order to get us to choose one of them. In fact, people sometimes choose an option they like *less* in order to avoid being pressured to make a certain choice by manipulation of the utilities.

But if the options have not been manipulated for someone else's benefit and under perfect knowledge, the comparative utility of the options to each other may not affect the level of freedom. But in the real world, since utility is uncertain, it is important that it be the actor who decides what the comparative utilities are, even when the utilities have not been manipulated. Clearly, if the comparative utility of the options is as it is because of the presence of a bribe or because one of the alternatives was set up to manipulate us, our level of freedom is lower than it would otherwise be.

Pressure can be applied to a choice situation in different ways and to different degrees. A person can be *prevented* from doing something (but allowed to do other things) or can be *forced* to do something. Degree of threat and of bribe have already been mentioned. Also, the probability that this threat or bribe will actually be carried out is relevant.

Negative utility can also be applied to a situation and in different ways. For example, if the environment I am in is suddenly invaded by musical sounds that I do not at the moment want to listen to, I am less free. I am forced either to endure the less desirable environment or choose another one (if there are any). Another example is the person forced to endure environmental pollution and unable to stop it or escape it. Also, I can be interrupted in other ways, asked a question, etc. If someone else forces a choice situation on me, thereby deciding when I shall choose, I am less free than if I decided when to choose.

Finally, if the threats or bribes are of unknown utility I may be less free than if the utility is known. Similarly, if these threats are attached, not to specific commands but to unspecified and ubiquitous prescriptions and proscriptions, a person is in a situation of an extremely low level of freedom. For example, a junior manager who works for an irrational and unpredictable boss is sometimes in this situation, as are children with inconsistent parents.

Similarly, people who are weighed down by the number of alternatives available, the amount of information available, the amount needed, and their limited ability to acquire, assess and make inferences from the information are less free than they would be if they could handle these factors and reach their decision easily. In addition, people under such conditions would probably try to avoid decisions in the future, thus further lowering their level of freedom. These conditions affect the "decision-making costs."

Rawls says that "lack of means" does not affect liberty itself but only affects the value of liberty to the person. However, people with lower levels of liberty may well value their liberty more, not less. In any case, the notion of worthless liberty has been dealt with in the first chapter.

Other philosophers restrict the list of abilities to be considered relevant. For example, Benn & Weinstein say that whether a person who falls into a pond far from shore and lacks the ability to swim is "unfree" depends on whether it is a "standard expectation" that everyone will be given the opportunity to learn to swim; in contrast, a stranded motorist "is neither free nor unfree but simply unable to attend." What they are afraid of, presumably, is that someone might propose legislation requiring the government to finance swimming lessons, etc. But no one is claiming that the government can or should do everything possible to increase freedom. That would be financially impossible. To restrict the definition of freedom because of the size of the government budget is a curiously backward way of proceeding.

In the present analysis, the definition of resources is unrestricted and includes things like amounts of time, money, space, other materials, number of other people cooperating with the person in question, as well as internal resources like skills, interests, health, mental and physical ability (absence of handicaps, for example), and so on. Any of these can affect the availability and utility of the options. (The effect of the availability and utility of the options on the level of freedom has already been discussed.)

Moreover, it does not necessarily follow from this analysis that rich people are always more free than poor people, since other factors than money must be considered. This too is an empirical question and is not built into the definition.

The number and utility of options in a given situation is also a function of the dependability of the courses of action or states of affairs that constitute the options, the length of a person's planning horizon, and the probabilities of various events of positive or negative utility occurring to improve or to ruin a future situation.

Does a high level of freedom require a precarious future or a dependable future? One's alternative courses of action must be dependable—the consequences must be as expected, but these consequences must not be such that they leave little viable choice in the future. The longer a person's planning horizon and the more dependable the options, the more free the person is, even in the present situation.

The probability that a situation will be or become less free would seem to be a function of the number of persons or other factors that are capable of applying pressure to a choice situation or decreasing the utility of a situation and the likelihood that they will actually do so. It would seem also to be a function of the number or proportion of actions or situations to which they can do this (and the probabilities that they actually will. These probabilities would have to be combined with the degree of utility of the various possible interferences. A person who might receive orders backed up by mild threats from three people is more free than the same person would be if the same orders were backed up by severe threats from the same people.

But other people may also be helpful and they may increase the level of freedom: by providing alternatives that would not otherwise be available, by providing information, or by improving the utility of a situation. Hence, as the probability of these occurring increases, so our level of freedom increases. For example, people who buy products that we make provide us with the option of continuing to make them. Also, friends who invite us to visit them at their vacation home offer us attractive options, thus rendering us more free.

Analogous considerations apply to the probability associated with such help. The number of persons or factors that might help by providing alternatives or information or improving the utility of the situation, the number of options or situations they might so affect, and the degree of utility of their help are all factors that affect the level of freedom of a situation.

Another consideration peculiar to helpful behavior, however, is the non-zero probability that it may be manipulative, that it is really intended to influence us or that it may lead to consequences that are not in our interests. These possibilities decrease the level of freedom that we have while faced with an offer of help. It would seem that if the offer stems from shared interests our level of freedom is greatest (other things being equal). For example, if friends extend an invitation whose acceptance would please them as well as us, or if two persons are exchanging something valuable to them both. When the offer is charitable, it may not last or may not recur, and when the offer is self-interested only, it may have unknown disadvantages or side-effects present or future or may decrease our future freedom (for example, it may make us dependent on someone who may become an antagonist). These factors must be considered along with the others in determining how free we are in situations in which options or information is provided by others.

It has been argued that the definition of freedom presented in chapter two cannot be adequate since it is really a definition of power, not a definition of freedom. It makes freedom and power have equivalent meanings.

The refutation is simple: freedom to do **x** implies the power to do **x**; but having the power to do **x** does not imply having the freedom to do **x**. A person with the power to land or not land a plane at Havana, Cuba may not be free to do so, if he has a gun at his back.

The ordinary word "power" usually refers to extraordinary feats. Hence, it would sound curious to say that freedom implies power. A person high in freedom might not be a very powerful person in a society. If the things a person wants to do require very little power (e.g. read, listen to music), then the person could be highly free but (in general) low in power.

A related argument: it does not sound odd to say that John does not have the power to jump over the moon. But it does sound odd to say that John does not have the freedom to jump over the moon.

However, one could argue that both statements sound a bit odd. But the odd flavor tells us nothing about the meanings of these words. It does tell us something about the state of our knowledge and of our technology. In the past, the standard example was flying to the moon. But now that flying to the moon is possible, that statement does not sound odd, so we change the example. The oddness derives from what is possible and tells us nothing about even the connotations of the words power and freedom.

Additional arguments over limiting freedom

Much has been written about limiting liberty from John Stuart Mill to the present. Some comment on this work is therefore in order.

Review of the Literature

The classic criterion for deciding the question of limiting freedom is, of course, J. S. Mill's "harm principle." Many objections have been raised to the harm principle; however, it is possible to substitute a similar but more general criterion which is not vulnerable to these objections. In addition, many believe that Mill went too far in never allowing a person's own good to be a grounds for limiting her or his freedom. But it will be shown below that attempts to refute this position have failed. To begin with, however, there is a criterion which Mill did not treat and which is perhaps the criterion most often presupposed in actual policymaking: that in order to have the benefits of collective action, individual liberty may justifiably be decreased. I believe that there is a mistake in the way this opposition has been set up.

Limiting Liberty for Collective Benefits

The expression "collective benefits" is being used here to include all cooperatively produced options, including most consumer products, as well as hospitals, parks, roads, knowledge, laws, etc. The production of such benefits requires some degree of organization (including not only industrial and service organizations but also contracts, the economic system and the legal system). It is evident that by providing options, such arrangements tend to increase the level of freedom. In fact, Dewey says "…there is no effective or objective freedom without organization." And even if this statement is a bit extreme, it is clear that the level of freedom will depend on the type of organizations and what they provide and fail to provide. But it is equally clear that organization often tends to constitute a decrease in individual liberty, though how much of a decrease evidently varies with the type of organizational design. Not all alternative collective benefits result in the same degree of decrease in or limitation of individual liberty.

It is usually assumed that if some degree of collective benefits are going to result from a project, it is justifiable to reduce individual freedom to obtain them. Although, the question how much collective benefit for how much individual liberty is rarely asked. But would it not be more reasonable to hold that a proposed collective benefit should result in a *net increase* in level of freedom rather than a decrease? Most collective benefits eliminate some options but create others. Only if people prefer the set of options created to the ones eliminated is the collective benefit justified. Moreover, use of this criterion does not mean that individual well-being is being sacrificed for the sake of freedom, since freedom, being the extent to which a person can do or have whatever he or she wants whenever she or he chooses, covers all the utilities that the person has and adds the condition that the control of these utilities is in his or her hands. Thus, a certain level of freedom implies a certain level of well-being or "happiness."

But why not approve a policy or collective benefit that provides higher benefit but lower freedom? For one thing, if a person does not have control of the source of the benefit, then even if benefits are high today, they may not be tomorrow. Moreover, if others control the benefits, they could use this control to control the person. Finally, some things that have benefit today may decrease the level of freedom tomorrow. Given these difficulties, it may be wondered how even the benefit could be high under such conditions. But a person might not be aware of the possible future loss or decrease in level of benefit (for example, the notion of the happy slave).

A further problem is that, for most collective benefits or organizations, the people whose level of freedom increases may not be the same people as those whose level of freedom decreases. Some people may prefer the options gained to the ones lost while other people prefer the options lost to the ones gained.

Hence, we specify that there must be a net increase in level of freedom for each and every person whose freedom is affected by the law, policy, organization or other collective benefit.

At first sight, such a condition may seem impossible, but it can be met if collective benefits or pieces of legislation are considered in sets or packages. The goal is to formulate policies such that, for all persons **A,** any decrease in the level of freedom of person **A** from project **x** is more than offset by an increase in freedom of **A** from project **y**. Only a criterion such as this will be in accord with everyone's interests. (In practice, some of the benefits may have to take the form of "compensations" to individuals, but here "compensation" is measured by increases in their level of freedom, not by a sum of money.)

When the problem of the trade-off of individual options lost for options gained due to cooperation or organization is formulated in this way, and the criterion of net increase in level of freedom is used, the normative problem is no longer to justify limiting liberty in cases involving collective benefits. The goal is to find what set of societal arrangements (social, political, economic, and legal) results in the highest level of individual freedom and what policies lead toward such arrangements. In other words, a given set of collective benefits must not only increase every person's freedom but increase it more than any competing alternative set of collective benefits. Otherwise, the set of collective benefits in question constitutes an unjustified limitation of individual liberty.

The problems that remain are formidable, but they are empirical problems, not normative ones, and are of the same order of difficulty as other problems in evaluation research. Still, given the methodological problems involved here, it may be necessary to fall back upon a piece-meal approach: for example, any existing or proposed law, policy, or feature of society could be challenged by showing that it results in less freedom for some individual than an alternative arrangement. Proponents could modify their proposal to remove this objection. Opponents could then seek another counterexample. The measurement problems here are still substantial, and the placement of the burden of proof (on the status quo or on the alternative) is too important to be settled by convention or postulation. Each side must present its case.

On a somewhat more general level, some particular piecemeal questions that can be asked (and that it is the task of empirical research to answer) are: (1) What aspects of organization or cooperation tend to increase individual liberty, that is, increase the resources that enable people to do what they want or that provide options that people may want, and/or decrease the pressure or manipulation they are under, or the psychological limitations that they have? And (2) What aspects of societal structure tend to do the opposite? Any claims that a particular law, policy or particular features of organizational design tend to do the one or the other could be formulated as structures of causal hypotheses and one could begin to test them, using whatever measures of level of individual freedom, however crude, can be designed. The results here also imply (for the reasons given above) that researchers who are now attempting to measure "welfare" should be attempting to measure level of freedom instead.

It is worth noting in this connection that, since level of freedom is the extent to which people are able to engage in actions (or be in situations) which have high utility for them, level of freedom implies level of utility or level of happiness. Hence, the existence of higher levels of unhappiness implies lower levels of freedom. Since the existence of unhappiness is easier to detect than levels of freedom, this relation has consequences for measurement. And since this is true, wide-spread unhappiness can no longer be justified with the claim that it is a result of freedom and that it is better to have freedom than to have happiness.

Collective benefits of all kinds, then, are not grounds for limiting liberty, but, if justified, are a means for increasing it.

Limiting liberty to prevent harm to others

John Stuart Mill in his classic essay allowed only one criterion for limiting liberty, what is now called the "harm principle:" "the sole end for which mankind are warranted, individually or collectively, in interfering with the liberty of action of any of their number…is to prevent harm to others." One of the problems with Mill's statement is the specification of what constitutes harm; hence, there are as many criteria here as there are definitions of harm. And some definitions of harm seem to limit liberty too much; others not enough. This statement of Mill also suggests that if any limitation of liberty occurs, it should always be the actor's freedom that is limited.

But consider the type of situation involved here: one person wants to do **x**, others want their experience not to contain **x** or its consequences. If the first person cannot do **x**, then her or his freedom is limited. But if the first person does **x**, then the others cannot have what they want and thus their freedom is decreased or limited. We are faced here with the freedom of two parties, not of one; and there is a conflict of liberties. The question that we must ask, then, is: According to what criteria do we decide whose liberty should be limited and by how much?

Limiting liberty for own good: paternalism

Some people have argued that the fact that the future consequences of a person's choice may be disastrous shows that freedom is not a good thing. People would be better off if some knowledgeable and benevolent person made their decisions for them.

Such an argument has most cogency when applied to children and parents. To apply it to adults has the obvious problem that the decision-making expert may not in fact be benevolent or may not remain benevolent. And the paternalist argument when applied to parents has to be qualified by the fact that parents typically do not have very much of the relevant knowledge and the fact that most of what needs to be known about child-rearing is not known by anyone.

In general, some authors have argued that the limitation of liberty for a person's "own good" is at least sometimes justified, a position which has come to be known as "paternalism."

But what "own good" means in this context must be the person's benefit in some other sense than the person's freedom: to limit a person's liberty today because this is the only means whereby the person can have a maximum level of liberty over the time period which includes the future as well as today is to appeal to a principle of maximum liberty, not to a principle of limitation of liberty for the sake of some other good, since the practice alleviates limits to freedom rather than increasing those limits.

The usual "hard cases" or cases in which previous authors have thought paternalism justified (such as those characterized by the actor's ignorance, emotional states, compulsion, mental illness, irrationality, and so forth)are cases in which the level of liberty of the actor is low and will predictably become even lower unless a temporary interference with freedom is made now by other people. But the appeal in these cases is to minimizing the decrease in liberty or in other words to maximum overall liberty. Unless some cases can be found, then, that are based on some other principle than maximum liberty, "paternalism" in the sense of limitation of freedom for the sake of other personal benefits than freedom has not been shown to be justified.

The problem that remains, however, whether called "paternalism" or not, is still substantial. Perhaps this can be shown by contrasting this application of the criterion of maximum liberty with its application in the first alleged grounds for limiting liberty discussed above (viz. eliminating some options in order to obtain more highly desired options provided by cooperation): the difference is that in the present case, it is alleged that the locus of decision-making must be outside the person or persons whose freedom is being temporarily decreased (or some of whose options are being eliminated).

But why would a locus of decision outside the person result in the person's being more free? It would seem that one would have to show (a) that if some decision is not made, the overall level of freedom of the people in question would not be maximized, and (b) that the decision-maker has the capacity to make a decision that would maximize their freedom, and (c) that the capacity of the people in question could not be raised far enough or soon enough to enable them to make the decision themselves, and (d) that the decision-maker is trustworthy enough and altruistic enough to actually make the decision on the basis of the benefit of the people in question.

It may rarely be possible to meet such a large number of conditions. Obviously, there would be less overall limitation of the freedom of a group of people if their capacity were increased than if the decisions were made for them. Also, for example, if intervening each time a child is about to hurt himself or herself results in the child developing a dependent personality, the child would be more free overall if some or all of these interventions were omitted. Thus, "paternalism" may often be unjustified even where children are concerned.

But neither can we say that one person can never intervene in someone else's behavior in such a way that the other's overall freedom is increased. If there were unalterable physiological limits on the capacity of the actor (brain damage, retardation), or if there were time constraints (emergencies, infancy), or if the means necessary to maximize freedom made inclusion of the actor in the decision-making self-defeating (as sometimes perhaps in psychotherapy or in the military secrecy necessary for defense), it might be possible to increase overall freedom by a temporary intervention.

But one would have to include in the comparison of levels of overall freedom the power of other people or enforcement agencies, since this power might enable them to carry out limitations not authorized by the above conditions, and this danger would exist as long as the power existed. How great this danger is will vary with the effectiveness of the self-regulatory capabilities of the society and of the individuals who occupy the decision-making positions in question.

The problem

Where do the limits to a person's liberty in fact come from? First, there are the limits arising from nature. People cannot spread their arms and fly, they cannot travel from coast to coast in one minute, etc. These limits can be and have been decreased by technological means. In any case, they present a purely technological problem, not a normative one.

Second, there are limits arising from societal arrangements or the sharing of resources. This limit has already been discussed under "Limiting liberty for collective benefits" above.

There remains, then, the limits resulting from other people's actions, in other words from conflict.

But clearly if one person's conduct is not decreasing someone else's freedom, this question ought not to arise. A preliminary question that must be asked, then, is: Under what conditions is a person's freedom in fact being limited by the actions of others?

Presence of conflict

The following criterion may be suggested: The freedom of one person can conflict with the freedom of another only when there is some form of sensory contactbetween them, direct or indirect, present or future. Unless an action or its consequences make some form of sensory contact with other people at some time or other, the others are not forced to see it, hear it, etc. and thus are not forced to think about it. They may think about it and may indeed become very upset over it, but only if they themselves choose to do so. The actions of the former, then, do not limit the freedom of the latter. Hence, the question whose freedom to limit ought not to arise.

But if one person's present action makes sensory contact with someone else in the future, then it is not ruled out by this criterion. Another person's conduct, though unseen by me, may affect me later or may have an indirect effect on me. For example, the person who drops the proverbial banana peel that I slip on or the person who pays someone else to injure me.

However, not all cases of sensory contact constitute conflicts with or limitations of anyone's liberty. They do so only if they change the priorities of the various options that a person has (especially the priorities of the most preferred options), since they thereby put pressure on or manipulate the person's choice. If I have chosen to use the reading room of the library even though the room is too warm and someone lowers the temperature to a more pleasant level, this action has made sensory contact but has not limited my freedom.

Dealing with conflict

The ultimate goal of society is the maximization of the liberty of each and every individual person in the society. As far as conflicts are concerned, therefore, the ultimate goal is to prevent conflicts from occurring and to eliminate or dissolve them when they do occur.

Preventing conflict

Conflicts can be minimized or prevented by having *reserved spaces* for certain *activities* (for example, study areas, recreation areas) and by having reserved spaces for *people* in which areas they can do whatever they like (for examples, homes) and by having reserved *objects* for people which they can use whenever they want.

The latter satisfy two of the senses of "privacy." Having reserved spaces for people prevents conflict by reducing sensory contact. Having reserved spaces for activities helps to prevent conflict by insuring that the contact that does occur does not interfere with the chosen activities. This policy resembles the "rights" approach to liberty, but in the present approach there is no need to postulate these arrangements as rights a priori.

Conventions and laws also make behavior more predictable and thus make it possible for people to make choices which avoid some conflicts when alternatives exist. (This is not to suggest that laws and norms are unproblematic.)

The level and frequency of such conflicts and hence of the level of freedom that individuals typically have in a society will vary with the extent to which those who are in contact with each other like the consequences of each other's actions at the same times, and with the extent to which the number of things they dislike is minimized. This does not imply that policies encouraging conformity or even similarity are best, since people are also sometimes attracted to people who are different from themselves and since liking the same things could lead to bottlenecks and scarcity. But often liking the same things will decrease the likelihood of conflicts. In addition, socialization practices which increase the number and intensity of dislikes that people have increase the likelihood of conflicts and lower levels of freedom.

Other methods of preventing conflicts undoubtedly exist and should be sought.

Dissolving conflict

Sometimes the conflict can be eliminated by one or both or all parties choosing to go to reserved areas, if they have any. Another solution is to provide such alternatives. For instance, where homes having certain characteristics are available to all individuals, some reasonably desirable alternatives will always be available and thus conflicts will be less serious than they would otherwise be. (This may not be true for young people who do not have their own reserved spaces at home.) Similarly, when a certain level of resources is available to people, they will be more likely to have some alternative which is not too much less desirable than the one which is in conflict.

Another possibility is modifying the places themselves to reduce conflicts. For example, in the case in which one apartment dweller wants to play music while the resident of another apartment wants to read, it may be possible to minimize overall limitation of freedom by constructing apartment buildings such that they are soundproof, have separate air circulation systems, etc.

In sum, it could be suggested that the criterion to use is overall level of liberty, not merely the change in degree of freedom produced by the situation at issue. It is possible, for instance, to construct situations in which most of the actions that **A** is interested in are blocked for one reason or another, or situations in which **A**'s level of liberty is much lower than that of other people. Should **A**'s freedom be further limited in the conflict situation at issue? It is clear that such injustices should be corrected. But allowing some people to hurt others is not the way to correct them. Rather, levels of liberty should be raised by other means. Hence, a comparison of overall levels of freedom between **A** and **B** is the criterion to use to resolve conflicts in which an action of **A** produces unwanted consequences for **B**.

Notes

The Crisis in the Meaning of Freedom

Fuller, Lon, "Freedom: A Suggested Analysis," *Harvard Law Review* 68, no. 8 (June 1955), p. 1305.

*After all, liberty…*I am using "freedom" and "liberty" interchangeably. The question whether these should be two concepts or one is one of the questions the present discussion is all about.

*life, liberty and property…*Property being necessary to sustain and guarantee the other two.

Montesquieu, C., *The Spirit of the Laws*, 1748, Book 11, ch. 3.

Rousseau, J-J., *The Social Contract*, 1762, Sk. I, ch. 8.

*one of the battle cries of the revolution…*They tried, but ten amendments had to be introduced immediately before some states would ratify the U.S. Constitution.

Mill, John Stuart, *On Liberty*, (London: Longmans, 1859).

Mill, J. S., *ibid.*

Basset, R. J., *The Essentials of Parliamentary Democracy*, London: Macmillan, 1935, p. 110; cf. also Duncan-Jones, A. "Freedom to Do Otherwise," *The Cambridge Journal*, III, 754 (1950).

Scott, K. J., "Liberty, License and Not Being Free," *Political Studies*, 4: 182 (1956)

Oppenheim, Felix, *Dimensions of Freedom*, St. Martin's Press, 1961, pp. 170-172.

Orwell, George, *1984*, Harcourt, Brace, 1949.

And people could never defend their freedom to do x, since opponents could always claim that doing x exceeds the limits to freedom. Also, of course, lack of a theory of limits makes it impossible to defend claims that a person's freedom should be denied in any specific case. But somehow, contrary to past tradition, the present assumption seems to be that the burden of proof is on the person who would claim freedom rather than on the person who would limit it. This placing of the burden of proof is especially dangerous when limits on freedom are placed piecemeal rather than in accordance with a theory of limits, since in principle each act would have to be justified separately and this in itself would be a constraint on liberty.

Buchanan, J. *The Limits of Liberty* (Chicago: University of Chicago Press, 1975).

Berlin, Isaiah, *Four Essays on Liberty* (Oxford: At the University Press, 1969).

von Hayek, F. A., *The Constitution of Liberty* (Chicago: University of Chicago Press, 1960).

MacCallum, G. Jr., "Negative and Positive Freedom," *Philosophical Review* 76 (July 1967); Blackstone, W. T., "The Concept of Political Freedom," *Social Theory and Practice* 2, no 4 (1973).

Feinberg, J., *Political Philosophy*, Prentice-Hall, 1973.

Friedrich, Carl J., ed., *Liberty: Nomos IV* (New York: Leiber-Atherton, 1962).

Oppenheim, *op. cit.*

Berlin, Isaiah, *Four Essays on Liberty* (Oxford: At the University Press, 1969) p. 122.

Scott, K. J., *loc cit.*, pp. 182-183.

Oppenheim, F. E., *op cit.*, p. 69.

Scott, K. J., *loc cit.* p. 183.

von Hayek, F. A., *The Constitution of Liberty* (Chicago: University of Chicago Press, 1960) pp. 12-13.

No one wants to be committed by a theory of liberty to requiring the government to regulate cave-ins or to pass laws governing falls into crevasses. Actually, governments do change the physical landscape, for example, by building roads, etc. And some of these changes increase the liberty of a lot of people. Whether government does it for the purpose of increasing individual liberty or to make it possible for people to get to stores more easily and thus improve business is a moot point.

people sometimes give the label "free" to their experienced condition even when they can't do very much of what they want to do. Draughon, W. E., unpublished empirical research, 1976.

useful as a touchstone to test the relevance of any proposed dimension of the concept of liberty. I am omitting some of the more bizarre definitions of freedom, since I do not think they are likely to influence public policy in the near future.

One definition equates freedom with death: when one dies, one becomes free. To make freedom so defined a goal of public policy would lead to a curious society, for example, one in which search-and-destroy squads were sent around to shoot everybody on sight, thus making everyone free.

Another definition has it that freedom is having nothing left to lose. Strictly speaking, this means that the free person is dead, otherwise he would have his life to lose. But one assumes what is meant here is having no material possessions to lose. Certainly there are a few people who make a living sponging off other people, but to make free riding a goal of public policy would result in everyone being a sponge, in which case there would be no one to sponge off, and everyone would die of starvation.

Richard Lovelace (1618–1658), "To Althea, from Prison".

Oppenheim, F. E., "Degrees of Power and Freedom,", *American Political Science Review*, 1960; and *op. cit.*; Berlin, I. *op cit.* p. 130, footnote 1.

Draughon, W. E., "Conditions on Level of Freedom", *Psychology*, (May, 1978) vol. 15, 2, 51-55.

What Freedom Is

Some of the material in this chapter originally appeared in *Social Theory and Practice*, vol. 5, no. 1 (Fall, 1978) pp. 29-44.

David Hume, *An Enquiry Concerning Human Understanding*, Sect. 8, pt. 1, Art. 73; John Dewey, *Human Nature and Conduct* (New York, NY: Modern Library, 1950), 309; H. J. Laski, *A Grammar of Politics* (Reading, MA: Allen & Unwin, 1925), 144; Lon L. Fuller, Freedom: A Suggested Analysis," *Harvard Law Review 68*, no 8 (June 1955); I. Berlin, *Four Essays on Liberty* (Oxford: At the University Press, 1969), 130; S. W. Forbes, "Freedom and Organization Reconsidered," *American Journal of Economics and Sociology 31*, no. 2 (April 1972): 189-98.

John Locke, *An Essay Concerning Human Understanding* (1690), Vol. 1, Bk II, Ch. 21, Sec. 7-13.

The test then will be whether the difference in the situations makes a difference as to how free *the person is in the two situations.* A variable does not have to make a difference at every level or for every configuration of values of other variables in order to be relevant to freedom. If there exists such a configuration and the person is more free for one value of the variable in question than for another, then the variable in question is relevant to freedom. Put in the terminology of Analysis of Variance, we shall be searching for the existence of interaction effects.

The justification will be carried out later. The statements in the analysis are intended as descriptive statements, and most of them are in principle intersubjectively researchable; but the descriptive analysis as a whole is put forth as a proposal. The proposal that this set of conditions be taken as a definition of liberty and thus as a goal of society is a prescriptive statement.

We are assuming that the person in this situation does not care *what the thickness of the paper is.* And we are ruling out by stipulation the fact that a real person in a real situation would still be free to *think* whatever she wanted to think.

Suppose you have two options: you can have your arm pinched or you can have your toenails pulled out one by one. Your choice. Some readers might think of the possible counterexample of masochism at this point. Obviously, I am trying to provide examples at this point to illustrate the basic conditions. More complicated conditions are introduced as we proceed. In particular, I deal with depth-psychological factors in the chapter on conditions.

John Stuart Mill, *On Liberty* (Longmans, 1859), chapter 5.

We can either watch one program we like or watch another we like. If you think about it, the unavailability of all your desired activities is a good general definition of imprisonment (or lack of freedom). Consider an extreme case in which all you wanted to do is to read. If this were all you ever wanted to do, you would not be imprisoned if locked in a room with immediate access to any book in the world, while if locked *out* of the only library in the world, you *would* be imprisoned.

Jonathan Swift, *A Tale of a Tub.*

This behavior provides a clue that Bill is probably deceiving himself about his valuation of classical music. In general, there are eight methods that can be used to make the discrimination between actual valuation and perceived valuation: (1) how much time the person spends doing the allegedly valued activity, (2) how much the person is willing to pay (or give up) in order to have the valued activity, (3) how strong an obstacle the person is willing to (and actually does) overcome to experience the valued activity, (4) whether the person fantasizes about the allegedly valued activity or looks forward to it, (5) how much regret the person experiences when the allegedly valued activity is no longer available, or conversely how much relief the person experiences, (6) how long the person remembers the activity and how vivid the memory is, (7) the actual perceived experience of elation while doing the activity, (8) whether the prospect of doing the activity "pulls us" toward it, or whether we have to "push ourselves" to do it.

What all this shows is that when we make decisions, we are taking, usually a smaller, but sometimes a greater risk. Generally, the degree of risk decreases our level of freedom. But some people find risk-taking exhilarating. For them, the amount of risk tends to increase their level of freedom. But as the degree of risk increases, there will be a point at which the level of freedom decreases. All of which is not to say that these points can be precisely measured. The point here is to illustrate some of the complexities that affect the level of freedom for different kinds of people.

R. B. Perry, "What Does It Mean To Be Free?" *Pacific Spectator 7* (1953).

Fuller, 1324; Forbes, 189; Steiner, C. Perceived freedom. In L. Berkowitz (Ed.), *Advances in experimental social psychology*. vol 5. New York: Academic Press, 1970, Pp. 187-248.

Draughon, W. E., "Beliefs About the Nature of Freedom," *Psychological Reports, 42*, pp. 767-770, 1978.

Dewey, *Human Nature and Conduct*, p. 303, p. 304.

R. F. Ladenson, "A Theory of Personal Autonomy," *Ethics 86* (1975): 30-48.

if the only other alternatives were mildly interesting to them…However, the actual, as opposed to the perceived, level of freedom may have to be measured against what the person would want to do under perfect knowledge and unlimited resources.

we want to be able to think *freely*. Aren't thoughts always free? Counterexamples are hard to find; but one can imagine, for example, an extremely obsessive man who could not get a particular thought out of his head; he would be more free if he had a choice of thoughts. Such depth-psychological factors are discussed in more detail in the chapter on conditions of freedom.

How far we look ahead depends on our knowledge of the consequences of the options and how important we think those consequences will be. Sometimes the "spontaneous" person does not look ahead at all. If she is lucky, the consequences will be benign. The time and effort involved in looking ahead are known as "decision-making costs" and, like all costs, count against our level of freedom. And at the other extreme, some people expend far more time and effort in choosing than the consequences are likely to be worth. The optimally free person will know when it is appropriate to be spontaneous and when it is too dangerous.

Limiting Freedom

our major problem would be to provide a justification for these rules.
Many theorists in twentieth-century meta-ethics have argued that justification of moral rules is in principle impossible. It is not possible here
to recapitulate the arguments used to try to establish this conclusion.
See any competent textbook on the subject, for example, Garner, Richard T. and Rosen, Bernard, *Moral Philosophy*, MacMillan, 1967.

*Attempts to justify a set of moral rules have appealed to the acting per-
son's own good and to the advisability not to harm other people.* Other
arguments appeal to special knowledge available from supernatural
sources. The problem with these arguments is that it is not possible to
establish the existence of these supernatural sources. We are advised to
take them "on faith." But this begs the question. The question we are
asking is: to what set of rules or principles should we give our faith?

*…implementation will always remain impossible, then we will have to
rule out that proposed solution…* On the other hand, if we can approach
closer and closer to a proposed resolution, and such a resolution is the
best we can do, we may admit that resolution.

For anyone knowledgeable of computers, we can point out that this
problem is essentially the same as that of time-sharing the CPU in
operating systems scheduling designs.

Freedom and Justice

Most of the material in this chapter originally appeared as "Beyond
Justice," in *Public Affairs Quarterly*, vol. 1, no. 3, July 1987, pp. 91-
101.

*Because of facts like these, some people hold that justice means making
the wage fit the job, paying higher wages to some people than to others.* Not
everyone accepts these arguments, of course. Some people hold that
every worker gets the job he or she wants, and therefore we can ignore
the characteristics of the job itself. There are people, they claim, who
simply love to clean toilets. In this best of all possible worlds, we need

not worry about the quality of the job. (The number of people who hold this view tends to be small, since the number of people who get the job they want tends to be small.) At the other extreme, there are people who feel that they have to suffer through their job every day, and other people can jolly well suffer through *theirs* too. In other words, all jobs are equally bad. But if this were true, these people would be indifferent between doing the job of janitor and doing their own job (provided the wages were the same). Faced with such a choice, however, people quickly change their tune.

Kelbley, Charles A. "Justice and Goodness" in C. A. Kelbley, ed., *The Value of Justice*, New York: Fordham Univ. Press, 1979.

What is due a person could be specified in the quantities one person receives relative to what another person receives or relative to a job the person does or relative to some other criteria of deserving. If the concept of "just due" is given a moralistic interpretation, we have the problem of justifying the morality. This morality may be particularly suspect if it requires the withholding of something people value from them.

Hume, David, *An Enquiry Concerning the Principles of Morals*, ed. L. A. Selby-Bigge (Oxford: Clarendon, 1894) pp. 183-189, and Rawls, John, *A Theory of Justice*, Harvard Univ. Press, 1971, pp. 126-130.

Hume, *loc. cit.*; Rawls, *loc. cit.*; Galston, William A., *Justice and the Human Good*, Univ. of Chicago Press, 1980; and Hubin, D. Clayton, "The Scope of Justice," *Philosophy and Public Affairs,* **9**, #1, 1979, pp. 3-24.

*If people can be persuaded that an attitude of infinite wants...*Economists and mathematicians assume that utility functions are infinite; but psychologists would, I think, question this assumption. At any rate, it is not obvious that human wants are necessarily infinite.

cf. Lafollette, Hugh, "Licensing Parents," *Philosophy and Public Affairs,* **9,** #2, 1980, pp. 182-197; and Hurka, Thomas, "Value and Population Size," *Ethics,* **93,** 1983, pp. 496-507.

cf. Schwartz, Adina, "Meaningful Work," *Ethics, 92*, 1982, pp. 634-646; and Sankowski, Edward, "Freedom, Work, and the Scope of Democracy," *Ethics, 91*, 1981, pp. 228-242.

The ideal, the ultimate goal of society, then, is plenty (satisfaction) for all people as soon as possible for as long as possible. The justification of the claim that this should be the ultimate goal is presented in the next chapter; for the present, this claim will have to remain putative, although hopefully it is intuitive as well.

In order to reach this goal, the benefits of society must be distributed and they must be distributed to everyone. Note that we are dealing with human beings with finite life spans. It would do no good to plan to have a person arrive at the goal sometime after her/his death. The extent to which people approach the goal is the extent to which they have plenty between the present time and the ends of their lives. Any other planning time for any given human being is absurd.

And if the jobs were of equal interest, competition might focus on the education or training that is required to qualify for the various jobs, the easiest educational route being preferred. One could distribute at random or bypass the issue by using the method used at present in our society: multiple distributing organizations which distribute to individuals according to their respective comparative market power. How favorable this arrangement is to the individuals who receive the income depends of course on the vagaries of supply-demand conditions. To justify this method, it would have to be shown that *all* individuals would be moved toward their satisfaction levels faster than they would be by any other method. Such a demonstration seems unlikely to be forthcoming. Hence, we need a criterion for producing the distribution or at least for testing it.

With these intermediate goals society does not need a concept of distributive justice. Neither this ultimate goal nor the concept of justice says anything about what proportion of society's resources should be devoted to shared benefits (e.g. roads, parks, etc.) as compared to individual benefits (e.g. consumer goods). But this decision depends so much on individual personality, individual tastes, that it is not clear that any general criteria *could* provide any guidance to this decision.

An intermediate goal of inequality addresses an ultimate goal of satisfaction for some as soon as possible. Whether creating exorbitant wealth is the most efficient way to stimulate investment is at least a point worth arguing about. There may be other ways, short of a full-scale planned economy whereby investment could be generated.

Schwartz, *loc. cit.*; and Sankowski, *loc. cit.*

Nozick, Robert, *Anarchy, State, and Utopia*, Basic Books, 1974.

It is to say that the goal is to produce a society that will make justice irrelevant. To say what the *goals* should be, limits but does not determine what the *means* should be to reach these goals. Several alternative means (political-economic systems) may be effective. The constructing of such means requires theoretical ingenuity, but the testing for effectiveness is an empirical problem, not a normative one, once the normative test criterion is given.

One of these is of interest only to philosophers and is presented in a footnote. Justice has always been the paradigm example of a concept that has had to be justified "deontologically," in other words, in some way other than on its merits. Liberty, everyone could see, was valuable. But justice was something, perhaps disagreeable, that people must accept anyway, out of charity toward other people in the society or as a hedge against the possibility of being one of those people oneself. But I have argued that the problem with the usual concepts of justice is not that they must be justified "deontologically," but that they cannot be justified at all.

Why We Should Accept This Definition of Freedom

The justification that I will be offering, then, will be neither a deductive proof nor a preponderance of empirical evidence. I am not claiming at this point that the support I offer is a general theory of justification such that justifications of the same type could be offered for other (justifiable) normative claims. It would be nice to develop such an abstract theory in the future, but at this point I think it would be premature.

To put it another way, if you don't have a justifiable theory of liberty, your attempts to justify it should fail. The converse does not hold, of course: you may have a justifiable theory of liberty, and yet through lack of ingenuity your attempt to justify it may fail.

Skepticism is incoherent. This point is elaborated in a paper, "The fundamental question of ethics" (in preparation).

that each person's own or "self-regarding" interests are (part of) the ultimate goal of society... Or, to make it explicit that this is a normative statement: that each person's self-regarding interests ought to be adopted as (part of) the ultimate goal of society. The reason the qualifier "part of" is inserted is that these individual interests must still be aggregated and conflicts between them resolved. If these interests were not the elements that make up the ultimate goal, then the question of aggregating them and resolving conflicts between them is moot.

Hence, the difference (though not the distinction) between self-regarding and other-regarding breaks down. What has been shown is that self-regarding and other-regarding reasons cannot be said to have no overlap whatever. Obviously, there are cases where a person's self-interest conflicts with the interests of others. These problems of conflicts of interests are addressed in the chapter on Limits of Liberty. The point here is that, as a basis or foundation for the present concept of liberty, self-interest cannot be shown to be objectionable on the charge of ignoring the interests of others.

In other words, there are self-regarding reasons for doing other-regarding actions. There is a caveat to note here: There is a distribution problem involved: people doing things for other people may result in some people receiving more favors or receiving better favors than other people and some people may receive no favors at all. To illustrate by an extreme case: everyone could do things for Jones. In this case, only Jones is better off, and doing such things would not be in anyone else's interest (unless they happened to like Jones and enjoyed doing things for him). In practice, however, absence of reciprocity tends to make other-regarding actions dwindle to zero, especially with regard to the person who does not reciprocate.

Witness Ivan Illych's moment of insight as he is dying: "What if my whole life has been a mistake?" Tolstoy, Leo, *The Death of Ivan Illych.* The fact that it was arguably not a morality that Ivan Illych followed all his life but another set of normative statements does not detract from the example as an illustration. The point is that following a set of pre-scriptions has a cost associated with it.

*Can there be good rational...*Recently, philosophers have attempted to attack the concept of rationality itself as used in decision theory on the basis of a game known as the Prisoner's Dilemma. (cf. Campbell, R. & L. Sowden, eds. *Paradoxes of Rationality and Cooperation*, Univ. of British Columbia, 1984, and the works cited therein). This attempt does not work. In the Prisoner's Dilemma, each person is deciding in a situation of uncertainty, uncertainty of what the other person will do; and communication cannot remove that uncertainty since the deci-sion-makers cannot assume that the other person is telling the truth.

The point is that even a rational person, acting under uncertainty, can make a mistake. You do not have to go to the Prisoner's Dilemma to show that. If you are hungry, it is rational to decide to go to the store to buy food. You do not know that a mugger will kill you on the way. Given your information set, it is still rational to decide to go to the store. If you had perfect information, you would decide not to go. If the two decision-makers in the Prisoner's Dilemma knew that the other had perfect information, they would know that they couldn't defect without the other knowing it; hence, they would both choose the alternative that would give them the more acceptable punishment. The temptation to defect and get a better payoff would be removed because they would each know that the other knows what they will do. The point is not which set of assumptions is more realistic. As long as information is uncertain, people will make mistakes. The point is not that rationality is "incoherent" or that there are two or more definitions of rationality or anything of the sort.

Again, this does not beg the question since no deductive relation is being asserted between the statement of costs and the theory T. The aggregation of individual liberties and self-interests into societal policies still has to be done and conflicts between these self-interests worked out. But again, it has to be done in such a way that the individual cannot be better off by adopting some other normative prescriptions.

Paternalism is perhaps the only challenger to democracy that remains under serious consideration today. For example, another possible challenger could be the claim that the individual people in a society are not what matters. What matters is the great achievements of the society: the great buildings, or the great works of art, or the great military victories or whatever. Such positions as these are not discussed much anymore because they are so easy to refute. The argument would run as follows: why are the achievements of this society great? Any attempt to answer this question will be a value judgment and one will have to justify that value judgment. Of course, if all the people in the society take pride in these beautiful buildings or whatever and prefer to have them than to have a few more comforts for themselves, then that is no problem—but then, such a situation becomes equivalent to (or could be justified by) the present theory of freedom: every individual prefers this situation and has chosen it. In all other cases, the attempt to justify the claim that these achievements are great breaks down: we simply have the value judgments of some people being imposed on other people.

Plato, *The Republic.*

Mill, John Stuart, *On Liberty*, Longmans, 1858.

In order to make the social system resilient, resistant to tampering, the people in the society have to share the responsibility for maintaining it. This is the "self-regulation problem."

cf. Draughon, "Beliefs about the Nature of Freedom," *Psychological Reports*, 42, 1978, pp. 767-770.

cf. Draughon, *loc cit.* as well as unpublished research on this point.

Conditions That Make Us More Free

Moreover, having many such good experiences together increases the value of the other person. I do not deal explicitly with cases like the fact that going through a bad experience together sometimes brings people closer together (in other words, makes them value each other more), but I am not denying these cases either. In fact, it is not really such a different case. The experience in question is a sharing or enduring of the painful experience together. And this sharing is a positive experience. When the other person did not cause the painful experience, we experience the pain and do not like it, but we also experience the companionship and we appreciate it even more, especially if the other person is undergoing it voluntarily for our sakes.

In that case, the enhanced value of experiences shared with this other person does not occur. An exception to this is a situation of competition (such as a sport). Sometimes the negative value of the other person (the competitor) actually increases the value of the shared (competitive) activity.

A threat *is someone else saying, "If you do **A**, I'm going to make sure the consequences are bad."* A threat can be distinguished from retaliation. In retaliation, the promise of bad consequences is attached to your doing harm to the other person. In a threat, the promise of bad consequences is attached to your failure to do something that benefits the other person.

In other words, this is not a choice, there is an element of force applied to the choice situation itself. A bribe is only relevant to level of freedom if it changes the priority of one of the options in such a way that that option competes with the highest priority option. If you have decided to go to college and someone offers you a bribe if you will go, the bribe does not affect your level of freedom. Similarly, if you have decided to go, and someone offers you ten dollars to stay home, it probably does not affect your level of freedom (assuming you are not desperately in need of money).

A bribe *is someone saying, "If you do **B**, I'm going to make sure the consequences are good."* This has been called "compensatory power" by Galbraith, J. K., *The Anatomy of Power,* Houghton-Mifflin, 1985.

De Crespigny, *loc. cit.;* R. Price, "Dr. de Crespigny on Coercion and Freedom," *Political Studies 16,* no. 3 (1968): 433-36; D. M. White, "Power and Liberty," *Political Studies* (March 1971).

But if someone says, "If you sell me your wife, I'll pay you a million dollars," we would usually consider this a bribe. Such an incident was actually reported in the press. A rich Arab offered to buy an American man's wife. According to the account, they compromised, and the Arab rented her for the summer for a million dollars.

John Holt, *Freedom and Beyond* (New York, NY: Dell, 1973).

J. R. Pennock and J. W. Chapman, eds. *Privacy* (New York, NY: Liber-Atherton, 1971).

Some of the material in this section originally appeared in *Psychological Reports*, 46, 1980, pp. 1251-1260.

Christian Bay, *The Structure of Freedom*, (Stanford: Stanford University Press: 1958).

See A. Bandura, "The self system in reciprocal determinism", *American Psychologist 23* (1978) 344-58.

M. Goldfried & M Merbaum, eds., *Behavior change through self-control* (New York, NY: Hold, Rinehart & Winston, 1973).

Albert Ellis, *Reason and emotion in psychotherapy* (New York, NY: Lyle Stuart, 1962) 82.

But the image these people seem to have of the human personality does not correspond very closely to any theory in psychology, not even Freud's, the one usually cited. Or perhaps I should say "sighted," because the literary people who cite Freud usually seem not to have read him and to be "sighting" him from afar.

Not every personality theory posits unconscious processes...A conspicuous and respectable example of one that doesn't is George A. Kelly, *The Psychology of Personal Constructs*, Norton, 1955.

M. Milner, *On Not Being Able to Paint* (New York, NY: International Universities Press, 1957).

A. Lowen, *Depression and the body* (New York, NY: Coward, McCann & Geoghegan, 1972) 28.

Eric Fromm, *Escape from Freedom* (New York, NY: Rinehart, 1941) 258.

Abraham Maslow, *Motivation and personality* (New York, NY: Harper, 1955) and Henry Murray, *Explorations in personality* (New York, NY: Oxford University Press, 1938).

David Braybrooke, "Let needs diminish that preferences may prosper," in N. Rescher. ed., *Studies in moral philosophy* (Oxford: Basil Blackwell, 1968) 86-107.

R. Wicklund, *Freedom and Reactance* (Potomac: Lawrence Erlbaum Associates, 1974).

W. Mischel & H. Mischel, "A Cognitive Social-learning Approach to Morality and Self-Regulation," in T. Lickona, ed., *Moral Development and Behavior* (New York, NY: Hold, Rinehart & Winston, 1976) 84-107.

Milton Rokeach, *The Open and Closed Mind* (New York, NY: Free Press, 1960).

Theodore Adorno, D. Levinson, E. Frenkel-Brunswick & R. N. Sanford, *The Authoritarian Personality* (New York, NY: Harper, 1950).

Bay, 1958.

B. Collins, J. Martin, R. Ashmore & L. Ross, "Some dimensions of the internal-external metaphor in theories of personality," *Journal of Personality 41* (1973) 471-92.

Otto Rank, *Will therapy and truth and reality* (New York, NY: Knopf, 1945).

Stanley Benn, "Freedom and Persuasion," *Australasian Journal of Philosophy 45* (1967) 256-75.

See B. F. Skinner, *Beyond Freedom and Dignity* (New York, NY: Knopf, 1971).

Bay, 1958.

*However, a psychological theory that postulated no executive function-
ing, no decision-making, would be incompatible with freedom...*such as
Skinner's.

von Hayek, op. cit.

*Nonetheless, if freedom is being able to do what you want to do, and if
what you want to do costs money, you are free to the extent to which you
have the money to do it.* The relation between freedom and money,
however, is not linear, for several reasons: Not everything you want to
do costs the same amount of money. Moreover, once you have enough
money to do what you want to do, having additional money does not
raise your level of freedom very much. Money is, of course, always a
hedge against future unforeseen contingencies.

Walker, George Lee, *The Chronicles of Doodah*, Houghton-Mifflin,
1985.

*What actions you should take is therefore open to considerable contro-
versy.* And it is beyond the scope of this book to discuss or to try to
resolve that controversy. See the economic literature for discussions of
these issues.

de Jasay, Anthony, *Social Contract, Free Ride*, Oxford University
Press, 1989.

Applying the Theory to the Real World

*Now the task is to come up with a design for a society that satisfies those
constraints.* Putting that design into practice by getting legislation
passed, etc. could also be called "implementation." Actually carrying
out the programs (the "implementation" in my sense) is called "implementation" in evaluation research. See Peter H. Rossi, Howard E.
Freeman, Sonia R. Wright, *Evaluation: A Systematic Approach*, Sage
Publications, 1979.

How free is he is these situations? Specialists will be thinking by this
time that a lot of "dirt" has been "swept under the rug" by the theory
of liberty presented here. It is all very well to say that this theory is in
the interests of every individual person, but haven't you ever heard of

Pareto optimality? Aren't you aware that there are conflicts of interests? One state of society might be in the best interests of one person while a different state would be in the best interests of another person. Jones would like to have it all and leave Smith with nothing; Smith would like to have it all and leave Jones with nothing. How can you sit there and blandly talk about a society that is in everyone's best interests!

All of this is true. Unfortunately, a society that is set up only to benefit Jones is not one that can ever be justified to Smith. (Smith can be drugged or deceived or hoodwinked or persuaded to vote for it, but Smith acting as a rational person would never do so.) So, dreams of one-person Utopias are beside the point. The problem here is to come up with a society that is, as far as practicable, in *everyone's* best interests.

Faced with a choice between a society in which neither they nor anyone else gets very much, people would probably prefer to modify some of their own interests to get a society they would like better. Our problem is thus more general than the game theorist's problem. Our utility functions can be changed.

Any temptation that any of them might have had to feather their own nest will be pointless. In this way, the research project accomplishes in a realistic setting what Rawls tried to accomplish by positing an imaginary "veil of ignorance." (Rawls, *A Theory of Justice*, Harvard, 1974) But here, it is accomplished without resort to metaphysical or imaginary veils.

A model of an individual, for example, would include what the person wants, the relative priority of those wants, the person's options for satisfying those wants, and the conditions affecting those options. The model will not assume that the people who are to be in the society are ideally rational people, nor that they are utility maximizers, nor that they have perfect information. It is to be a society for real people. The model may include plans to help people to become more informed and more rational, however. The model will also not assume that all the people in the society are cooperative. In fact, it will explicitly contain provisions for dealing with people who are not.

The model will contain tens of thousands of variables. Models to simulate the entire U. S. economy have already been built at M.I.T.

It may require fundamental changes in the model which render useless many of the refinements that have been put in. If this were a business project, the management would quite likely decide that too much had been invested so far to go back and start over again. The system will be sent out and fingers will be crossed that the special case that caused the undesirable results will never occur or at least will not occur for a few years, long enough to earn back the money already invested in the project. Needless to say, this is not the approach being proposed here.

a series of such group decisions might yield inconsistent results... This is of course the famous result proved by Kenneth Arrow and now known as Arrow's theorem.

There are a number of known problems that have been discussed in the philosophical literature. One is an approach known as "contractarianism." The approach assumes an imaginary situation in which people sit down across a bargaining table and agree on what their society is going to be like and agree on each group decision made in the society and agree on whatever interactions are to be held between themselves. In this way they arrive at a "social contract." Philosophers from Hobbes and Locke to John Rawls and David Gauthier have adopted this approach. Many of the criticisms of their work focus on the agreement situation itself, and game theory has been used to point out situations that might arise which make it at best paradoxical as to what choice the two people could make to maximize their expected utilities.

Since the approach taken in this book does not go about setting up a society in this way, it does not appear that the problems raised against contractarians apply to this approach. Also, some of these theorists want the outcome of these negotiations to satisfy some criterion of fairness. I have dealt with this problem in chapter 4.

These people are called Free Riders in the philosophical literature, but I prefer to call them by the name they call themselves, "Smart Guys." The free rider problem is a technical problem for my approach, not a theoretical or philosophical one. I make no judgment about the status of the problem for the contractarian approach. Anthony de Jasay in *Social Contract Free Ride* (Oxford University Press, 1989) holds that it is a serious problem for contractarians.

Any model worked out for a society to maximize individual freedom would have to make provision for some kind of policing function to keep the Smart Guys in check. This certainly limits the freedom of the Smart Guys. I don't see that it need put any serious constraint on other people (assuming the laws are reasonable) unless what they want to do is illegal. But I have no problem with, for example, limiting someone's freedom to cheat his neighbor. Certainly, the ancient problem "Who will watch the watchers?" is still a problem; and techniques like self-policing systems, checks and balances, etc. may not be sufficient to deal with this problem. New methods may have to be invented. But however difficult the problem, I see it as a technical problem, not a flaw that invalidates the theory of freedom presented in this book.

For Professional Philosophers

R. A. Wickland, *Freedom and Reactance* (Lawrence Erlbaum Associates, 1974).

Ibid.

Felix E. Oppenheim, "Degrees of Power and Freedom," *American Political Science Review*, 54 no. 2 (June 1960) 439-40.

Steiner, 195.

Oppenheim, *Dimensions of Freedom*, New York: St. Martin's Press, 1961, p. 117.

Wicklund, *Freedom and Reactance*.

Oppenheim, "Degrees of Power and Freedom," p. 438.

John Holt, *Freedom and Beyond* (New York, NY: Dell, 1973).

Fromm, Erich, *Escape From Freedom*, 1942.

Oppenheim, *Dimensions of Freedom*, 221; Eric Fromm, *Escape From Freedom* (New York, NY: Rinehart, 1941).

John Rawls, *A Theory of Justice* (Cambridge, MA: Harvard University Press, 1971), 204.

Benn and Weinstein, 436, 438.

Dewey, *Human Nature and Conduct*, 309.

Oppenheim, "Degrees of power and Freedom," 442.

Ibid. 441.

Steiner.

It has been arguedthat the above definition of freedom cannot be adequate since it is really a definition of power, not a definition of freedom. It makes freedom and power have equivalent meanings. By Sidney Hook, personal communication.

J. S. Mill, *On Liberty* (London: Longmans, 1859). Peter Radcliff, ed., *Limits of Liberty* (Belmont: Wadsworth, 1966).

James M. Buchanan, *The Limits of Liberty* (Chicago: University of Chicago Press, 1975).

John Dewey, *Human Nature and Conduct* (New York, NY: Modern Library, 1922; rpt. 1952) 306.

Russell Ackoff, *Redesigning the Future* (New York: Wiley, 1974).

Peter H. Rossi, Howard E. Freeman, Sonia R. Wright, *Evaluation: A Systematic Approach*, Sage Publications, 1979; Michael Quinn Patton, *Utilization-Focused Evaluation*, Sage Publications, 1978; Emil J. Posavac and Raymond G. Carey, *Program Evaluation: Methods and Case Studies*, Prentice-Hall, 1980; Elene N. Bernstein (Ed.) *Validity Issues in Evaluative Research*, Sage Publications, 1975; Terry Nichols Clark (Ed.) *Citizen Preferences and Urban Public Policy*, Sage Publications, 1976.

Nunnally, J. C. and Wilson, W. H. "Method and theory for developing measures in evaluation research", In E. L. Struening and M. Guttentag (Eds.), *Handbook of evaluation research*, vol. 1, ch. 9, Sage Publications, 1975.

John Stuart Mill, *On Liberty*, 9.

Gerald Dworkin, "Paternalism," *Monist 56*, no. 1 (January 1972) 64-84; D. H. Regan, "Justifications for Paternalism," in J. R. Pennock

& J. W. Chapman, eds., *The Limits of Law* (New York: Liber-Atherton, 1974) 189-210; John D. Hodson, "The Principle of Paternalism," *American Philosophical Quarterly 14*, no. 1 (January 1977) 61-70.

Hodson, 61-62.

*The freedom of one person can conflict with the freedom of another only when there is some form of sensory contact...*That is to say, one person can see, hear, feel, taste or smell the other person or the results of the other person's actions.

Carl J. Friedrich, "Rights, Liberties, Freedoms," *The American Political Science Review* 57, no. 4 (December, 1963) 841-54.

0-595-26619-3

www.ingramcontent.com/pod-product-compliance
Lightning Source LLC
Chambersburg PA
CBHW061405280526
45784CB00001B/377